Wonders of Morgan Dollars

E · PLURIBUS · UNUM

1881

by *Leroy Van Allen* June 2018

Leroy Van Allen

October 2011

George T. Morgan, 1910, Age 65
Engraver

Anna W. Williams
Model

Medal Room, Philadelphia Mint, 1901
George Morgan

Published by

Rare Coin Investments (RCI)
P.O. Box C
Ironia, NJ 07845

Copyright © 2021 by Michael S. Fey, Ph.D.

Authors: Leroy C. Van Allen and A. George Mallis

Library of Congress Catalog Number: 2023904390

ISBN

Printed in the United States

TABLE OF CONTENTS

Dedication

To the many collectors who continue to study and find so many new interesting things about the Morgan dollars.

INTRODUCTION

This document is a summary of the Wonders of the Morgan silver dollar for both the beginning collector and the more advanced collector. By Wonders, it is meant the unique features of the authorization of the Morgan dollar coinage, why so many were stored unused for decades, their current widespread availability in uncirculated condition compared to the contemporary subsidiary coinage, some amazing hoards that have surfaced over the years, it's beautiful design and appearance in the silver, and some truly unique and wondrous kinds of die varieties. The Morgan dollar was a common coin available from circulation and most banks up until the early 1960s when few collected it and there was little premium for most dates. Since then it has risen in the 1970s and 1980s to be the most widely collected and invested in the U.S. coin series and a dominant coin in the U.S. coin market because of it's availability in uncirculated condition.

The availability of the Morgan dollar was due to it's production and storage as back-up for the more popular and convenient paper money silver certificates. It was minted at the Philadelphia and San Francisco Mints from 1878 thru 1904 and again in 1921. Mintage occurred at the New Orleans Mint from 1879 thru 1904, at the Carson City Mint in Nevada from 1878 thru 1885 and again in 1889 thru 1893 and at the Denver Mint in 1921. Of the 570 million Morgan dollars produced from 1878 thru 1904, in 1905 about 455 million were held by the U.S. Treasury for payment of silver certificates with 40 million held in excess and only about 75 million were in circulation. That is the reason so many never reached circulation. But they did also serve a useful function in three U.S. Government crises: The **Pittman Act** that melted 270 million Morgan dollars into bullion during **WW I** to aid **Great Britain** in quelling a war emergency silver crisis and possible rebellion in India, the shipment of 13 million dollars of bullion from the Pittman Act supply and 29 million of Morgan dollars in 1919 & 1920 to **China** to end a silver speculation crisis there, and for emergency **silver bullion needs** during **WW II**, including the Manhattan Project, when 53 million silver dollars were melted.

Their appearance can also be a wonder because of their mintage in 90% silver. Since silver is the **most reflective** of all metals, the polishing of the dies resulted in many early strike coins having **mirrored** fields contrasted by **cameo** devices to make highly attractive and prized coins. Their large size at one and one-half inches in diameter coupled with a classic Liberty head design and eagle with very fine life-like engraved detail makes for an extremely attractive coin.

There are many amazing tales and stories of thousands and thousands of bags of Morgan dollars from the disposal of the Treasury silver dollar holdings up until early 1964 when their stock of silver dollars was depleted. An exhibit of **one million silver dollars** at the **1962 Seattle World's Fair** included 800 bags of 1,000 Morgan dollars with 200,000 1922 Peace dollars loosely poured around them that came from the Federal Reserve in Philadelphia at face value. Four million people saw the exhibit and 250 bags of Morgan dollars were sold at $1,500 each and the rest were sold back to the Federal Reserve bank at the end of the exhibit.

Later, silver dollar hoards surfaced including the infamous **Redfield** hoard of 400,000 silver dollars dispersed in the late 1970s, the **Government Service Administration** sale of three million **Carson City** Morgan dollars in the 1970s and early 1980s, the giant hoard of 1.5 million Morgan dollars of the **Continental-Illinois Bank** dispersed in the early to mid-1980s and the little known **Stansbury** hoard of over 750,000 uncirculated silver dollars quietly dispersed from 1966 thru 1985. Many other lesser hoards of Morgan dollars have been quietly dispersed over the years. No known uncirculated coin hoards of the contemporary Liberty Seated and Barber halves, quarters and dimes have ever surfaced that even remotely approached the quantities of these Morgan dollar uncirurlated hoards, since the subsidiary coinage was mostly released into commerce around the time they were produced.

But the primary thrust of this document on Morgan dollars is the wonders of the **die varieties** found on this large coin. There are over three dozen different kinds of die varieties summarized. With a 7X or 10X hand magnifying glass, a whole new world of wonders can be found on this large coin. Did you know that there was unauthorized use of **acid** in an attempt to repair around a dozen dies at the San Francisco Mint in 1878 and 1879? Or that the majority of the 1921 Morgan reverse dies have had **hand engraving** on the reverse eagle's right leg and in the wings in an attempt to fill in over polished areas. There are well over 30 **over date** dies for the 1880/79 P, O & S and two over date dies for the 1887/6 P & O. There are also three **over mint mark** dies for the 1882 O/S and five over mint mark dies for the 1900 O/CC.

There are hundreds of dies with **doubling** on the Liberty head portrait, eagle and peripheral lettering and stars including the spectacular 1888 O **Hot Lips** with doubled lips, nose and hair and the 1901 P **Shifted Eagle** with strongly doubled tail feathers. There are also hundreds and hundreds of **doubled date digits** since they were punched by hand into the dies from 1879- 1904, including large lateral and vertical shifts. Many **doubled mint marks** exist since they were all punched into the working dies by hand, and there are even some punched in crossways such as one 1879 O and one 1895 S.

Most of the 1878 P 8 tail feather reverse dies were **touched up by hand** to add small feathers at the bottom of both the eagle's wings to fill in over polished areas. Many 1878 S and some 1878 P and 1879 S dies were also **touched up with hand engraving** of a wing feather at the eagle's right leg to fill in an over polished area. In addition, a few 1878 S and 1879 S reverse dies had additional feathers engraved at the upper tail feathers to produce the interesting die varieties of **8 and 9 upper tail feathers** instead of the usual 7 tail feathers. And of course, there is the well–known **1878 P 7 over 8 tail feathers** dual hub dies with 13 dies of the 8 tail feathers design re-hubbed with the 7 tail feather design that produced dies showing 3 to 7 tail feather ends showing below the normal 7 tail feathers. There are even two known cases of **engraving on the Liberty head jaw** with one for an 1878 S die that produced a **Sagging Jaw** line and one 1904 O that has engraving lines on the jaw and upper neck.

A strange **dash** was below the right 8 on many dies from 1884 thru 1886 that served as an index mark for the punching in the date digits. Even stranger were over 50 dies that had the tops of date digits **punched into the denticles** below the date and even in the spaces between the date and denticles or above the date in the lower hair line. Apparently this was to test if a batch of obverse dies had been annealed before their dates were punched in.

Other weird marks that have showed up primarily on the reverse dies are **denticle edge impressions** of 6 to 8 raised dots in a line on dozens of the reverse dies. This was likely due to accidental contact of the edge of the obverse die with the reverse die face as they were being installed in the coining presses. Several reverse dies have even been identified as having been **used in two different years** to strike 1878 S coins and again for 1879 S coins.

The Morgan dollars have had their share of **counterfeit coins** including crude **cast coins** passed into circulation decades ago. There was a large counterfeiting operation around 1902 in the New Orleans area that produced the **infamous Micro O** and related counterfeit 1896 O, 1900 O, 1901 O and 1902 O die struck coins. To date, counterfeit 8 obverse cast dies 11 cast revere dies and 6 collars have been identified that produced a total of 20 die combinations. Up to possibly 10,000 counterfeit die struck coins could have been produced all having similar circulation appearances and casting defects. It is the largest counterfeiting of Morgan dollars uncovered to date. Key Morgan dollars dates of 1889 CC, 1892 S, 1893 S, 1894 P, 1895 S, 1901 P, 1903 S and 1904 S have all been counterfeited by **adding mint marks or altering the mint marks** and these dates should always be authenticated.

Special **identifying marks** in the form of **dots** have been added to two obverse and reverse dies of the 1884 P near the designer's initial M and below the eagle's wings for several reverse dies of 1921 P, D & S. Besides the 1878 P 7 over 8 tail feather dual hub dies as previously mentioned, other **dual hub dies** have been identified for the 1878 P 8 tail feather with **doubled eagle's beak,** over 30 1878 P obverse dies with **doubled LIBERTY** and other features, the many 1900- 1904 **two olive** reverse dies and the many 1901- 1904 **doubled Liberty head** profile.

Even the edge reeding has some interesting collar varieties including the **infrequent or wide**

reeding on some 1921 P. Some faulty made collars with **overlapping reeding** at one to three locations exist for some of the 1883, 1884 1892, 1900, 1901, and 1904 New Orleans struck coins.

The so-called **clashed 'E'** below the eagle's tail feathers on the 1886 O, 1889 O and 1891 O have been known since the early 1960s and are very collectable. When the obverse and reverse dies clash together without a planchet between them, parts of the opposite die design can be transferred. Die clash marks are common, but the scarcer **clashed letters** that have been transferred below the eagle's tail feathers, at the Liberty head neck and lower hair edges are very collectible. Hundreds of dies have been found with clashed letters, with the 1889 P clashed In at the neck an especially strong rare example.

Quite a few of the Morgan dies show **gouges** and **scratches** imparted on them before or as the dies were used. One of the earliest and strongest known die gouge is the 1890 CC **Tail Bar** with a wide gouge from the left tail feather down to the wreath. An amazing series of seven die gouges and die polishing sequences occurred on the 1921 S **Thorn Head** around and on the Liberty head. A couple spectacular die gouges on the late die state of an 1882 CC reverse die has only been recently reported in 2009. An 1878 S has a spectacular wide band gouge **across the top of the Liberty head**. The die with the largest number of die gouges, by far, with over **30** on the lower reverse die of an 1888 S **Monster Gouges**.

As the Morgan dies were used and wore out, they naturally accumulated breaks and chips. But some breaks are unusually large such as the 1888 O **Scarface** with a long die crack from the rim over across the Liberty head face with displaced field breaks. The 1887 P has a large break at the bottom right of D in DOLLAR on the reverse called **Donkey Tail** the was reported in 1964. An 1881 S reported in 1999 has a very **long vertical die crack** with wide breaks on the eagle from the neck down to the eagle's right leg and to the rim below D in DOLLAR. There are also a number of spectacular and **rare rim cuds die breaks** for the years 1889 O, 1891 O and 1921 P & D.

The Morgan dollar has the usual **planchet errors** such as rim clips, split planchets, laminations and impure metal streaks which can be pretty noticeable because of the coin's large size. There also exist a number of **striking errors** such as multiple strikes, broadstrikes, off-center strikes and weak strikes. But these and large planchet errors are fairly rare because of the individual coin inspections given the Morgan dollar from 1878 thru 1904. The struck thru foreign material, partial collars and rotated dies striking errors are all also fairly rare.

This has only been a brief over view of some amazing things that can be found on the Morgan dollar, especially the world of die varieties when viewed with a hand magnifying glass. The applicable books and articles that cover specific topics are given at the end of each section. It is hoped that this introduction to the large number of wonders of the unique Morgan dollars will encourage collectors to delve deeper into this amazing series.

Further available resources on the Morgan and Peace silver dollars are at these Internet web sites: VAMLink.com, VAMWorld.com, VAM-e.com, rcicoins.com, vamsandmore.com.
VAM refers to the first letters of the co-authors of Leroy Van Allen and A. George Mallis of the book, *Comprehensive Catalog and Encyclopedia of Morgan & Peace Dollars,* Worldwide Ventures, 4th ed. 1998.

Philadelphia Mint, 1833- 1901

Carson City Mint, 1875

Philadelphia Mint, 1901

San Francisco Mint, Circa 1890

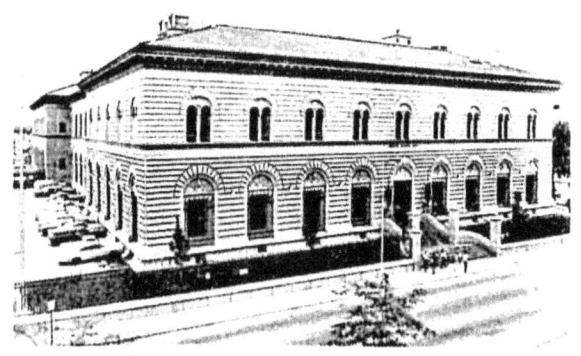

Denver Mint, 1906 to Present

New Orleans Mint, Circa 1890

Hand Magnifying Loupes

Stereo Microscope

THE COIN

This chapter treats the various **Acts** that **authorized** the production of the Morgan silver dollar, it's **appearance** that makes it so attractive to so many collectors, it's unique **availability** in uncirculated condition compared to other contemporary coins and the various interesting **hoards** that have appeared on the coin market in the 1960s thru the 1980s.

Authorization

Assistant engraver **George T. Morgan designed** the Morgan silver dollar as it is currently known. Earlier it had been known as the Bland silver dollar after the standard silver dollar legislation Bland-Allison Act sponsor in the House by Richard P. Bland. William B. Allison was in charge of the bill in the Senate. The **Bland-Allison Act** was passed by Congress on **February 28, 1878** over the veto of President Rutherford B. Hayes who pointed out that the then current market value of the silver in the proposed silver dollar was from ninety to ninety-two cents as compared with the standard gold dollar. The Act restored legal tender character to silver money and required the Treasury to purchase, at the market price, two to four million dollars worth of silver per month and to coin it into silver dollars. The Act also introduced a new kind of paper money into the U.S. currency, the **silver certificate**, which was widely accepted because they were readily converted into silver dollars. These silver certificates circulated in much greater amounts than silver dollars because of the latter's heaviness and bulk. As a result, most of the coined silver dollars were deposited in the Treasury and **stored in vaults unused**, but required by law as **backing for the silver certificates** that were issued.

The Morgan silver dollar was designed by Assistant Engraver George T. Morgan during the years 1876 through 1878 with many revisions and modifications to both the obverse and reverse designs. The approved design, in the words of Dr. Henry R. Linderman, Director of the Mint from 1873- 1879 was:

...the obverse of the coin bears a free cut head of Liberty crowned with a Phrygian cap decorated with wheat and cotton, the staples of the country,- the legend E Pluribus Unum, thirteen stars and the year of coinage. On the reverse, surrounded by an olive wreath an eagle with outspread wings bearing in his talons a branch of olive and a bundle of arrows– emblems of peace and war– the inscriptions 'United States of America' and 'One Dollar' and the motto 'In God We Trust'...

The **Phrygian cap** or Liberty cap originated in Phrygia and was worn by ex-Roman slaves to show they were free. Both the Liberty head and eagle show very fine detail. The Liberty head shows a good likeness of the model Morgan used, **Miss Anna Willess Williams** who was 19 at the time of the modeling sittings in 1876. That is one of the things appealing about the Morgan dollar is the **life-like** rendition of the **Liberty head**.

The **Sherman Silver Purchase Act** of **July 14, 1890** repealed the provisions of the Bland-Allison Act and required the purchase of $4,500,000 of silver per month to be paid for with Treasury notes and coin two million ounces of silver bullion into silver dollars each month until July 1, 1891. The **Treasury notes were redeemable in silver or gold**. Thereafter, only as much to be coined to provide redemption of the Treasury notes. Because the Treasury had high stocks of uncirculated silver dollars at that time, the production fell in 1891 and 1892. Congress **repealed the Sherman Act** on **November 1, 1893** because of a severe financial panic and the drain on the Treasury gold reserves because most Treasury notes were redeemed in gold. Coinage of Morgan silver dollars fell to low numbers during President Grover Cleveland's second term, 1893- 1897, because of his opposition to silver interests. An **Act of June 13, 1898** directed coinage into standard dollars all of the remaining bullion purchased under the Sherman Act which was completed in 1904 and coinage of the Morgan dollar ceased. From 1878 thru 1904, **570,272,610 Morgan dollars were minted** and even by 1918 over 400 million silver dollars were held unused in reserve.

On **April 22, 1918 the Pitman Act** was passed that directed that not more than 350,000,000 standard **silver dollars be converted into bullion** and sold at a price not less than $1.00 per fine ounce. It also authorized the purchase of a like amount of silver at $1.00 per ounce from American mine owners and the coining of the same number of dollars that had been melted. The **bullion was needed by Great Britain** to **quell a run on silver and possible revolution India** started by German war propaganda that the British government could not redeem the silver certificates for silver bullion in India.

Under the Pittman Act **270,232,722 standard silver dollars** (That is 270,232 bags of 1,000 coins!) were converted to bullion with around 198 million coming from the Philadelphia Mint and about 93 million from the San Francisco Reserve, but not all of these dollars were melted. No records of the year or mint of the dollars melted were kept, but most were likely uncirculated. Because almost half of the Morgan dollar mintage had been melted in 1918 and 1919, the **surviving number by date and mint differs greatly** in most cases **from the original mintage figures.** This is in contrast to the subsidiary coinage of the time that didn't have large melts and the mintage figures for them are reasonably accurate. Only the current supply and demand market prices indicates the true survival quantities of Morgan dollars.

In late 1919 and early 1920, 13 million dollars of silver went to the orient that was likely from the Pittman Act bullion. Also, **29 million Morgan silver dollars** (That is 29,000 bags of 1,000 coins!) were **shipped to China to counter a silver speculation bubble**, mostly in China, that had caused the price of silver to rise to nearly $1.40 per ounce by November 1919. The price of silver had to be brought down below the bullion value of $1.38 per ounce in subsidiary coins and $1.29 per ounce in silver dollars so they would not be hoarded and melted, thereby causing a crisis in the circulating coinage. By early 1920 the price of silver fell sharply to $0.70 per ounce and the crisis was over.

Because the **Pittman Act required** that the **silver dollars melted be replaced, 86,730,000 of the 1921 Morgan dollars** and 183,502,722 of the Peace dollars from 1921 to 1938 were struck. Under the Thomas Amendment and the Proclamation of 1933 additional 7,021,528 Peace silver dollars were minted in 1934 and 1935. A total of 53,029 Peace silver dollars were minted in 1934 and 1935 under the Silver Purchase Act and Proclamation of 1934. Under the **World War II Silver Act of December 18, 1942,** over **52 million silver dollars were converted to bullion in 1942 and 1943 for wartime uses**, including the Manhattan Project. It is not known whether the silver dollars melted during WW II were primarily Morgan or Peace dollars. Silver dollars were also **melted** from the early **1880s thru 1964** because they were **mutilated or uncurrent** and included Morgan dollars. A total of **333 million** silver dollars were **melted from 1883 thru 1964** under the Pittman Act, World War II Silver Act and mutilated coins, plus 29 million were sent to China during 1919 and 1920. In addition, **many millions** of **Morgan and Peace dollars** that were circulated and common dates **were melted in late 1979** and **early 1980** when silver speculation pushed the price of silver to nearly $50 per ounce. No records were kept of the quantities or date or mint that went to the melting pot.

Public Law 88-36 of 1963 stipulated that silver certificates could be exchanged at the Treasury of the United States for silver dollars **or silver bullion.** By **early 1964 the Treasury vaults were cleaned out of silver dollars** by speculators, dealers and collectors, except for about three thousand valuable Carson City bags that were sold later in the 1970s and 1980s by Government auctions. Silver dollars that had been available from most commercial banks ended shortly thereafter as the price of silver rose rapidly in mid-1960s to the $1.29 per ounce value contained in a silver dollar. The Treasury lifted its price for silver of $1.29 on July 26, 1967 and silver was traded as a commodity on the open market at $1.50 per ounce and higher beginning August 21, 1967. **Silver certificates went out of circulation** in the **late 1960s** and the Public Law 88-36 authorized the issuance of **$1.00 and $2.00 Federal Reserve Notes** to eliminate the need for silver as backing for these denominations.

As a result of all of these silver dollar melts, **less than one-half of the Morgan dollars** and perhaps three-quarters of the Peace dollars mintage remain. Although silver dollars were never widely used in commerce, they were **needed as backing for silver certificates.** Also, their **melting into bullion** helped to **quell a possible rebellion in India during WW I, provided emergency use during WW II** and the **shipment of large quantities** of Morgan dollars in **1919 and 1920 to China** that **put an end to a dangerous silver speculation.** Since 1964 these remaining magnificent silver dollars have resided with collectors and in dealer inventories.

Available references–

Comprehensive Catalog and Encyclopedia of Morgan & Peace Dollars, by Leroy C Van Allen & A.
George Mallis, 4th ed., 1998, WorldWide Ventures, Chapter 2, Silver Dollar Coinage.

The Comprehensive U.S. Silver Dollar Encyclopedia, by John W. Highfill, Highfill Press, 1992,
Chapter 6.

Silver Dollars and Trade Dollars of the United States, A Complete Encyclopedia, by Q. David Bowers,
Bowers and Merena Galleries, 1993, Chapter 13.

Did German Intrigue Cause Pittiman Act?, by Dwight H. Stuckey, *Coin World,* Nov. 13, 1985, pg 46.

Silver Dollar Melt Part of War Intrigue, by Dwight H. Stuckey, *Coin World,* November 13, 1985, pg 1.

George T. Morgan, Engraver, 1910, Age 65

George Morgan, Metal Room, Philadelphia Mint, 1901

William B. Allison

Richard P. Bland

Appearance

The Morgan dollar was one of the **largest U.S. coins** to circulate at one and one-half inches in diameter. The large size with easily visible design and letters makes them highly desirable to many collectors and investors. In addition, the **classic Liberty head** on the obverse with **very fine detail** on both the Liberty head and reverse eagle imparts a **conservative older look** coupled with **90% silver** composition that **implies value**. This silver composition allows detail and sharp features to be struck up compared to the modern copper-nickel clad coinage. The luster of silver is also more attractive.

Silver is the **most reflective** of all the metals. The basining and polishing of each pre-1904 Morgan dollar die provided a curvature on the die face that allowed even filling of the die detail across the coin. This also created **highly polished mirror-like fields** that usually lasted several thousand early coin strikings before the fields became dull from die wear. These Morgan dollars with **mirror-like fields** have been dubbed **proof-like** as they resemble the highly reflective fields of the specially made Morgan dollar proof coins issued each year in limited quantities. **Exceptionally deep mirrored fields** that reflect objects four or more inches are called **Deep Mirror Proof-Like (DMPL)** that are scarce and command considerable premiums.

There are also **frosted devices** that show up well on silver coins. This frosted effect is from the tooling on the master die that is imparted to the working hubs and working dies. Again, early struck coins can have the frosted devices or so-called **cameo** look until the working die frosting is worn smooth by the die wear. Not all dates have cameo frosted devices on the coins as this frosting on devices also wore away on the working hubs and master die as they were used and subsequently replaced. But to some, the **ultimate look** of a **business struck Morgan dollar** is one with **deep proof-like fields with cameo devices**.

It should be noted that the coin sculptured model of the designs from 1916 onwards were prepared with no intention of basining the working dies. Also, the designs were not retouched during the intermediate steps to prepare working dies. This resulted in the Peace dollar not having the proof-like fields of the Morgan dollar with a more rounded design edges, coarse detail and no frosting on the devices.

Many of the Morgan dollars show **colors** on the surface from tarnish of the silver and is called **toning**. There were 1,000 coins in the mint bags of silver dollars weighing 60 pounds. The cloth of these **canvas bags contained sulphur compounds which tarnished the silver dollars** if they were against the canvas bag undisturbed for a long time. Many bags sat in the Treasury vaults for many decades. This resulted in colorful toning on all or portions of a coin if it was partially covered by another coin. Beautiful **rainbow toned crescents or most of a coin** side are highly prized by collectors. In addition, Morgan dollars placed in a paper wrapper rolls of 20 coins could also be toned by the sulphur in the paper at the edges of the middle coins and over an entire side for the end coins. Cardboard coin albums could also tone the edges of coins.

1881 Proof Obverse

1880 S BU Cameo Obverse

1881 Proof Reverse

1880 S BU Cameo Reverse

1881 S Toned Lower Reverse

1883 O Rainbow Toned

1888 O Toned Bands

Proof Reverse

BU Proof-Like Reverse

Availability

Because of their size and bulk, the Morgan dollars were not very popular for general circulation. Instead, the paper **silver certificates were much more widely used**, with the **silver dollars serving as backup for payment of certificates outstanding** by law. For example, in 1905 the total coinage of the Morgan dollars as reported in the Annual Report of the Director of the Mint was 568,228,865. Of this, 454,864,708 was held in the Treasury for payment of certificates outstanding and could not be released into circulation. The amount held in the Treasury in excess of certificates outstanding was 39,779,821. The amount in circulation was only 73,584,336, or only 13% of the total Morgan dollar production from 1878 thru 1904, and of this probably many bags of uncirculated dollars were held by commercial banks.

Up until 1964 when the price of silver was advancing rapidly to the $1.29 per ounce value contained in a silver dollar, the Morgan and Peace dollars were available at face value from most commercial banks. A **run** on the **Treasury holdings of silver dollar bags in late 1963 and early 1964 cleaned out** the **remaining stock** of silver dollar bags, except for 3 million valuable Carson City Morgans held aside for later sales. **Silver dollars disappeared from circulation shortly thereafter** as the price of silver rose to $1.29 in the mid-1960s and to $2.00 per ounce by late 1960s when silver was traded as a commodity. All of the silver dollars were then in private hands of speculators, dealers and collectors.

The total stock of silver dollars of **568 million in 1905** was reduced by **29 million to China** in **1919 and 1920**, about **50 million in WW II** and another **possible 4-5 million** of **mutilated Morgan and Peace dollar** coins melted up thru 1964 to the **484,722,100 in 1964** when the Treasury had released them all into circulation (Except about 3 million Carson City dollars held back for later disposal). Of this, the **570 million pre-1904 Morgan dollars** produced was **reduced** by about **270 million** by the **melting in 1918 and 1919 under the Pittman Act, 29 million went to China in 1919 and 1920**, another **perhaps 4 million melted** from 1945 thru 1964 as mutilated coin and an unknown quantity of **Morgan dollars melted** as part of the 53 million melted for **World War II purposes**, of **perhaps 10 million more.**

Of the 86 million 1921 Morgan dollars produced and 183 million Peace dollars produced, perhaps about 15% each were melted during WW II, of about 13 million 1921 Morgan and 27 million Peace dollars melted for a total of about 50 million dollars melted during WW II. The total stock of silver dollars of about **480 million in 1964** is thus **estimated** to be about **250 million pre-1904 Morgan** dollars, **70 million 1921 Morgan** dollars and about **160 million Peace dollars.**

In 1957, about 235 million silver dollars were held by the Treasury and Reserve banks with perhaps one-third uncirculated 1,000 coin bags. About 250 million were in circulation, of which many millions were held by commercial banks in original uncirculated 1,000 coin bags. One could estimate that one-third government held dollars then were uncirculated or about 70 million coins and perhaps one-fifth of those in circulation were in uncirculated coin bags or about 50 million coins, for a total of around **120 million uncirculated Morgan and Peace dollars**. One could also estimate that one-third of these may have been **pre-1904 uncirculated Morgan dollars or about 40 million** and the rest of **uncirculated 1921 Morgan and Peace dollars of about 80 million**. The remaining silver dollars of about **360 million** would be in various **circulated conditions.**

Even with these **gross estimates**, that is a <u>tremendous</u> number of available Morgan and Peace <u>uncircualted coins</u> of the 1878 thru 1935 **compared to the subsidiary coins** that were mainly in circulation. The availability of these older silver dollar coins in uncirculated condition has resulted in a very large market around them. Only the market forces of supply and demand can sort out their availability and value by date, mint and in uncirculated and circulated condition.

Hoards

There were a number of hoards of the Morgan silver dollar that have surfaced over the years. The stashing of several bags of 1,000 coins in a mint bag was quite common in the 1950s and 1960s. But their bulk, 60 pound weight per 1,000 coin bag and cost of face value of $1,000 or more meant that few large hoards of 1,000 coin bags occurred. Three well known and publicized hoards were the GSA sale of the Carson City dollars, the Redfield hoard and the Continental-Illinois Bank hoard.

GSA Sales

As the Treasury holdings of silver dollars began to run out in early 1964, it was discovered that nearly **three million uncirculated Carson City** silver dollars of special numismatic value were in the small remaining inventory. These three million Carson City dollars were set aside and transferred to the General Services Administration (**GSA**) in 1971 to be sold at mail bid. More than thirty forms, cards and letters and labels were designed and produced. Millions of brochures and 100,000 posters were printed and distributed to the 40,000 Post Offices and nearly 60,000 banks, savings and loans and credit unions. Several special documentary movies were produced and shown on television. Three hundred and ninety two special coin displays of one each of the ten different Carson City dollar years for sale were fabricated and sent to various banks.

The 2.9 million Carson City dollars were transferred to the **U.S. Bullion Depository at West Point, New York in 1971** where the inspection, sorting and packaging operations were performed. All **uncirculated CC** and other mint silver dollars were packaged into **large plastic holders of single coins** and then placed in a **special velvet lined presentation case**. About **100,000 circulated Morgan and Peace dollars** were placed in a **mylar display packet** and enclosed in a carrying envelope. There were roughly **600 thousand to one million each** of the **1882, 1883 and 1884 CC**, about **150 thousand each of 1880, 1881 and 1885 CC**, **60 thousand 1878 CC** and about **5 thousand each of 1879, 1890 and 1891 CC dates**. Some of the GSA holdings were sizeable amounts of the original mintage with **85 percent** of 1884, **60 percent** of 1883 and 1885 and **50 percent** of 1881 and 1882 years.

There were **five mail bid sales** by the GSA between **1972 and 1974** and **two in 1980**. Total gross sales was **$107 million** with about **$10 million in expenses**. That was the largest sale of a U.S. coin series up to that time. The market value for many of the Carson City dollars dropped somewhat after the first sales but rebounded a few years late. Carson City dollars in the GSA holders are very much sought after now and command large premiums over their original GSA selling prices.

Available references–

The Comprehensive Catalogue and Encyclopedia of U.S, Morgan and Peace Dollars Silver Dollars, by Leroy C. Van Allen & A. George Mallis, FCI Press-ARCO, 2th ed., 1976, Chapters 8, 9, 10.

Comprehensive Catalog and Encyclopedia of Morgan & Peace Dollars, by Leroy C. Van Allen & A. George Mallis, 4th ed., 1998, WorldWide Ventures, Chapter 9.

Carson City Morgan Dollars, by Adam Crum, Selby Ungar and Jeff Oxman, Whitman Publishing, 2010.

Morgan Silver Dollars, by Q. David Bowers, Whitman Publishing, 2004, Chapter 6.

The Comprehensive U.S. Silver Dollar Encyclopedia, by John W. Highfill, Highfill Press, 1992, Chapter 12.

Silver Dollars and Trade Dollars of the United States, A Complete Encyclopedia, by Q. David Bowers, Bowers and Merena Galleries, 1993, Chapter 14.

Redfield Hoard

The Redfield hoard of Morgan and Peace dollars received much publicity in the middle to late 1970s. This hoard contained over **400,000 Morgan and Peace silver dollars** with **mostly S mint** Morgan and Peace dollars with some Carson City and Philadelphia mint Morgans. The exact quantities of dates and mint marks of the coins were never publicly released.

LaVere Redfield was a multi-millionaire who made a fortune during the depression in land speculation and oil stocks. He moved to near Reno, Nevada in 1935 and continued to invest in real estate in Nevada. Redfield distrusted the government and the banks and **preferred hard currency**. For several decades, he **accumulated silver coins in the basement** of a three story stone chateau in Reno. Most were bags of silver dollars of primarily S mints. He was not a collector of coins but rather an accumulator of hard assets. Redfield died in 1974 in Reno at the age of 76 and his wife died in 1981. His fortune was estimated to be between 70 and 200 million dollars with only a small portion of it in silver dollar coins. At the time of his death, authorities in charge of the estate and the Internal Revenue Service found 680 bags of mostly silver and gold coins hidden in the basement of his home behind false walls. There were over 407 thousand Morgan and Peace dollars with 351,259 of them uncirculated.

Court battles began immediately after Redfield's death with two contested wills that one was proven to be a forgery. So the estate went to his widow and niece. Stack's of New York was retained to make an apprisal of the numismatic items from October 1974 thru April 1975. Early in 1975, **A-Mark Coin Company** of Beverly Hills, California heard a rumor of a large coin collection of the Redfield estate and eventually signed an agreement to purchase the Redfield coin collection in January 19, 1976 at a private sale. Meanwhile, **Rare Coin Galleries** learned of the existence of the Redfield hoard and formed a joint venture with **Bowers and Ruddy**. They filed a bid of $6,501,156 for the coins. The probate court then ordered a **public sale** on January 27, 1976 which **A-Mark won with a bid of 7.3 million dollars**.

Suits were brought by A-Mark against the Redfield estate to re-instate the original private sale price and against Bowers and Ruddy and Rare Coin Galleries for intentional interference with the original contract. But these cases were lost because the probate court had the jurisdiction to vacate a prior order entered into by mistake that would have realized a lower amount to the estate.

A-Mark enacted a **three marketing plan** and three coin firms of **Paramount International Coin**, **Robert L. Hughes** and **John Love** were **designated as primary distributors** with signed agreements not to disclose the hoard contents or dispersal plan. **Paramount** packaged the dollars in sonic sealed **plastic holders** identifying the coin's grade and that it was from the Redfield collection. Redfield hoard coins were heavily marketed in the late 1970s with distribution into the early 1980s. Their primary impact was on the scarcer S mint dates because of significant quantities suddenly available. The promotion strategy overall stimulated the coin market and new collectors of dollars were added because of their availability.

Available references–
Comprehensive Catalog and Encyclopedia of Morgan & Peace Dollars, by Leroy C. Van Allen & A. George Mallis, 4th ed., 1998, WorldWide Ventures, Chapter 10.
The Comprehensive U.S. Silver Dollar Encyclopedia, by John W. Highfill, Highfill Press, 1992, Chapter 13.
Silver Dollars and Trade Dollars of the United States, A Complete Encyclopedia, by Q. David Bowers, Bowers and Merena Galleries, 1993, Chapter 14.

Stansbury Hoard

Little is known about the Stansbury hoard of silver dollars. "Curly" Stansbury of Long Beach, California amassed a large hoard of over **750,000 of uncirculated silver dollars** in the 1950s and early 1960s. He bought with discrimination and readily paid a premium for quality coins and was a buyer of semi-scarce dates as well as common bags. No inventory of his hoard has ever been published. But included were many Carson City coins that were primarily 1878 CC. There were also large quantities of 1878 P 8 tail feather dollars as well as 1878 P 7 over 8 tail feather dollars. This hoard was dispersed effectively and quietly over a period of about 20 years **from 1966 to 1985 by Superior Stamp & Coin Company**. Stansbury passed away around 1985.

Available references–
Silver Dollars and Trade Dollars of the United States, A Complete Encyclopedia, by Q. David Bowers, Bowers and Merena Galleries, 1993, Chapter 14.

1962 Seattle World's Fair Million Silver Dollar Exhibit

An early hoard was an exhibit of **one million silver dollars** at the **1962 World's Fair** in Seattle, Washington that lasted six months. It was a **promotion** of the **fair committee to sell souvenir metals** and the **Behlen Building Co.** to advertize Bohlen buildings. All of the silver dollars were purchased at face value from the Federal Reserve in Philadelphia and transported by two trucks escorted by Cadillacs donated by General Motors. **800 bags of 1,000 Morgan dollar coins** were stacked into the center of a circular Behlen corn crib enclosed in glass. Over and around the bags of Morgan dollars were **loosely poured 200,000 of 1922 Peace dollars**.

Individual silver dollars were offered in a World's Fair holder at $1.95 postpaid and the bags of Morgan dollars were offered at $1,500 per bag to be shipped after the exhibit closed. About four million people saw the exhibit and **250 bags of Morgan dollars were sold**. After the fair, the excess silver dollars were sold back to the Federal Reserve Bank. Behlen calculated that they ended up with a net profit of $15,000.

Available references–
More on the 1962 Seattle World's Fair Million Dollar Exhibit, The E-Sylum: Volume 13, Number 50, December 12, 2010, Article 19.

Redfield Collection Holders

GSA Carson City Presentation Case

Continental-Illinois Bank Hoard

The largest single private hoard of about **1.5 million Morgan dollars** after the final dispersal by the Treasury Department in the early 1960s was the **Continental-Illinois Bank hoard**. Before 1964 when silver coins traded freely in commerce, most banks also had supplies of silver dollars for customers. Some banks accumulated hoards of silver dollars as collateral for loans. The banks ceased to give out silver dollars shortly after the Treasury Department exhausted their supply of silver dollars in early 1964 and the price of silver rose shortly thereafter so that silver dollars were worth more for their silver content than their $1.00 face value.

The Continental-Illinois Bank of Chicago had holdings of about 1,500 bags of Morgan dollars when it experienced financial difficulties in 1982. **Ed Milas** of **RARCOA in Chicago** was contacted by the bank in 1982 to purchase the bags of silver dollars. There were about **1,000 bags** of 1,000 coins each of **uncirculated coins** and about **500 bags of circulated coins**. The Brilliant Uncirculated coins dated 1878-1904 with **most** of them **being 1878-1888** with a **lot of common S Mint coins**. The **quality** of the **BU coins were very high**, since most of them came from the bank in original mint canvas bags. Because of the long-term storage in canvas bags, many of the coins had **beautiful toning** on them. In general, the quality was far superior to those of the Redfield hoard since the Redfield bags of coins were thrown down a chute to his basement and some of these bags broke open and the coins were later shoveled up. The 500 bags of **About Uncirculated coins were 1878-1885** with **most** of them being **1879-1882 O-Mint** coins.

The purchase price or details of the transaction of the sale of the 1.5 million Morgan dollars to RARCOA by the Continental-Illinois Bank have never been made public. But estimates have put the value of the **transaction at around fifty million dollars**, far exceeding the 7.3 million dollars for the Redfield transaction. **Colonial Coins of Houston, Texas** and **SilverTowne of Winchester, Indiana** were selected to help disperse the hoard of silver dollars. The coins were marketed in a quiet and controlled way beginning in the **Fall of 1982 and continued well into 1885.** Colonial Coins handled about 500 BU bags of primarily **1879-1882 S-Mint, 1883-1885 O-Mint and 1885-1887 P-Mint coins.** SilverTowne handled at least 350 BU bags and 500 AU bags.

During the release of the Continental-Illinois Bank hoard, the coin market picked up from a depressed state in 1982 to a rising market thru 1985. Nice MS 65 common date Morgan dollars doubled and quadrupled in price by 1985. The demand for nice silver dollars was high and their availability actually fueled the increased activity. This large hoard of silver dollars was readily absorbed and prices increased substantially for quality coins.

Available references–
Comprehensive Catalog and Encyclopedia of Morgan & Peace Dollars, by Leroy C. Van Allen & A. George Mallis, 4th ed., 1998, WorldWide Ventures, Chapter 10.
The Comprehensive U.S. Silver Dollar Encyclopedia, by John W. Highfill, Highfill Press, 1992, Chapter 14.
Silver Dollars and Trade Dollars of the United States, A Complete Encyclopedia, by Q. David Bowers, Bowers and Merena Galleries, 1993, Chapter 14.

DESIGN TYPES

There were **four basic obverse design types** and **four basic reverse design types** used for the Morgan dollar. Design changes to the obverse were rather minor with three types used in 1878, the third type from 1878 thru 1904 and the fourth type only in 1921. Design changes to the reverse were more significant with three types used in 1878, the third type from 1878 thru 1904 with some dies of the second type used in 1879 and 1880, and the fourth type only in 1921. The obverse design types are designated with Roman numeral, of **I, II, III and IV** and the reverse design types with capital letters of **A, B, C and D**. The following sections summarize these obverse and reverse design types.

Obverse Design Types

I Type — Thin letters in LIBERTY with evenly divided rear portion of the ear.

> **Minor sub-types:** I^1 Incuse designer's initial M.
>
> I^2 Raised designer's initial M with two parallel vertical bars.

Used only for 1878 P 8 tail feather reverse type A and a couple 7 tail feather reverse type B dies.

II Type — Thicker letters in LIBERTY with unevenly divided rear portion of ear.

Used on all 1878 CC and S and some 1878 P with B & C reverse types.

Some 1878 P have dual hub II/I dies with very short inner ear fill and evenly divided rear portion of ear that were used with reverse types A, B/A & C.

III Type — Thin letters in LIBERTY with unevenly divided rear portion of ear and lines in wheat leaves. Date digits made smaller in 1884 onward.

> **Minor sub-types:** III^1 Wheat leaf end well below bottom of R in PLURIBUS. Point of neck above middle of denticle. Used on some 1878 P.
>
> III^2 Wheat leaf end close to bottom of R. Point of neck above denticle space. Used on some 1878 P and from 1879 to 1904.

IV Type — Eyelash missing, hairlines coarser, no line at jaw-neck junction. Many minor differences because of new master hub preparation. Compete date in master hub and die. Used only for 1921.

Reverse Design Types

A Type — Eight tail feathers.

> **Minor sub-types:** A^1 Raised eagle's beak with small engraved feathers between bottom of wings and legs, In touches wing.
>
> A^2/A^1 Hooked eagle's beak, In away from wing. (A^2 sub-type doesn't exist by itself.)

Used on early 1878 P with type I and II/I obverses.

B Type — Seven tail feathers, parallel arrow feathers, flat eagle's breast.

> **Minor sub-types:** B^1 Long center arrow shaft or nock. Used on some 1878 P, CC & S with type II & II/I obverse. (*See note below.*)
>
> B^2 Short center arrow shaft or nock. Used on some 1878 P, CC, most 1878 S and some 1879 S & 1880 CC with Type II, II/I & III obverses.

Some 1878 P have dual hub B/A with 3-7 tail feather ends protruding below normal 7 tail feathers that were used with some type II & II/I obverses.

C Type — Seven tail feathers, slanted arrow feathers, rounded eagle's breast.

> **Minor sub-types:** C^1 A of AMERICA close to wing. Bottom inner feather of eagle's right wing is rounded and not connected to wing. Used on some 1878 P with II/I and III^1 obverse.
>
> C^2 A of AMERICA close to wing. Bottom inner feather of eagle's right wing meets feathers with thin line between wing and leg. Used on some 1878 P with II & III^1 obverses.
>
> C^3 A of AMERICA away form wing. Bottom inner feather of eagle's right wing squared off and raised. Used on some 1878 P with II, II/I & III^2 obverses, and with III^2 obverse for some 1879 S & 1880 CC and all 1879 P, O, CC, all 1880 P, O, S, all 1881- 1899, all 1900 O and some

1900 P, S, 1901 P, O, S and 1903 O.

    C⁴ Large and wide rounded space between eagle's left wing and neck (as opposed to narrow space on C¹, C² & C³). Used with III³ obverse on some 1900 P, 1901 P. O. S, 1902 P, O, S, 1903 O, S, 1904 S and all 1903 P and 1904 P, O.

    A dual hub C⁴/C³ on numerous dies shows two olives on left side of olive branch and wide eagle's wing-neck gap. Used on some 1900 P, S, 1901 P, O, S, 1902 P, O, S, 1903 S and 1904 S.

D Type   Seven tail feathers, parallel arrow feathers, flat eagle's breast. Many minor differences because of new master hub preparation.

    Minor sub-types: D¹ 17 berries in right wreath. Olive branch is weak and shallow under eagle's right claw. Used on some early 1921 P.

    D² 16 berries in right wreath. Olive branch is full and raised under eagle's right claw. Used on most 1921 P and all 1921 D & S.

Note: **B¹** reverse sub-type with long center arrow shaft is known as the **long nock** because that end of an arrow has a notch for the bowstring. This B¹ reverse is not especially rare for the 1878 P & CC coins. But 1878 S with B¹ reverse and long nock is quite rare, especially in AU and uncirculated condition, for the nine known die varieties.

    The accompanying photographs show some of the obverse and reverse design types. There are two charts of the obverse and reverse design types drawn by Dr. Roland Girardet in April 2002 that shows the main features of each design type and sub-type.

Available references–

Comprehensive Catalog and Encyclopedia of Morgan & Peace Dollars, by Leroy C. Van Allen & A. George Mallis, 4th ed., 1998, WorldWide Ventures, Chapter 6, Descriptions of the Designs.

1878 Morgan Dollar 8-TF Attribution Guide, by Jeff Oxman & Les Hartnett, 3rd ed., 2004.

A Guide to the Varieties of the 1878 Carson City Morgan Dollar, by John Roberts, 2010.

1878 P 7 Tail Feathers Morgan Dollar Attribution Guide, by Leroy Van Allen, Revised November 2010.

1878 S Morgan Dollar Attribution Guide, by Leroy Van Allen & Craig Lickenbrock, Updated March 2009.

Long Nock- A Guide to the 1878-S B1 Reverse Varieties, by John Roberts, 2008.

1902 O Morgan Dollar Series Attribution Guide, by Alan Scott, 2010.

1904 O Morgan Dollar Series Attribution Guide, by Alan Scott, 2010.

Top 100 Morgan Dollar Varieties: The VAM Keys, by Michael Fey & Jeff Oxman, 4th ed., 2009.

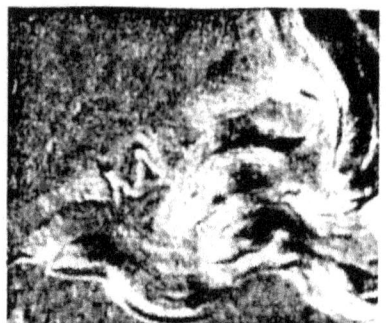

I 1 Obverse

I 2 Obverse

Type I Pointed Inner Ear Fill

Type II Blunt End Inner Ear Fill

II/I Short Inner Ear Fill

Type I Obverse LIBERTY

Type II Obverse LIBERTY

II Over I Obverse LIBERTY

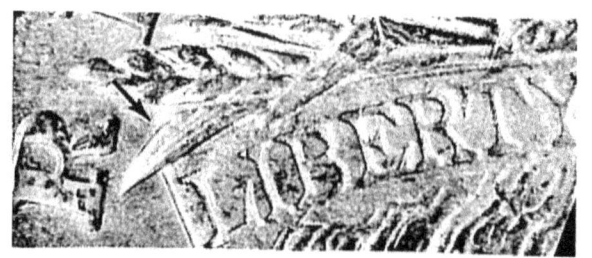

Type III 1 Obverse LIBERTY

A¹ Reverse

A²/A¹ Reverse

B¹ Long Nock

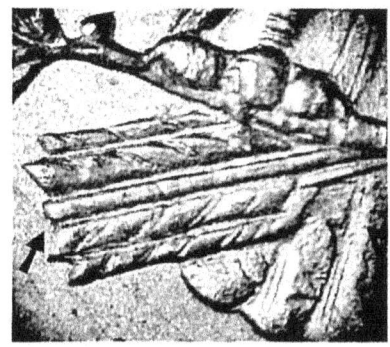

B² Short Nock

C¹ Shallow Feather Next To Leg

C² Line Next To Leg

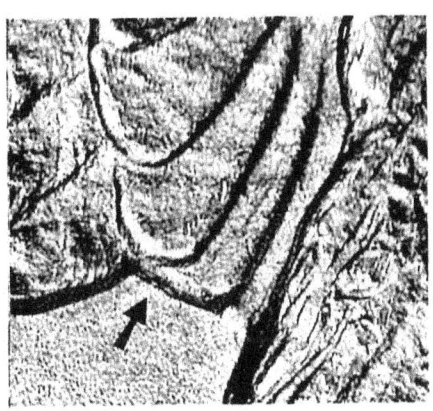

C³ Square Raised Feather Next To Leg

17 Berries D¹ Reverse

Dollar – Morgan: 1878-1921   Design Types: Obverse

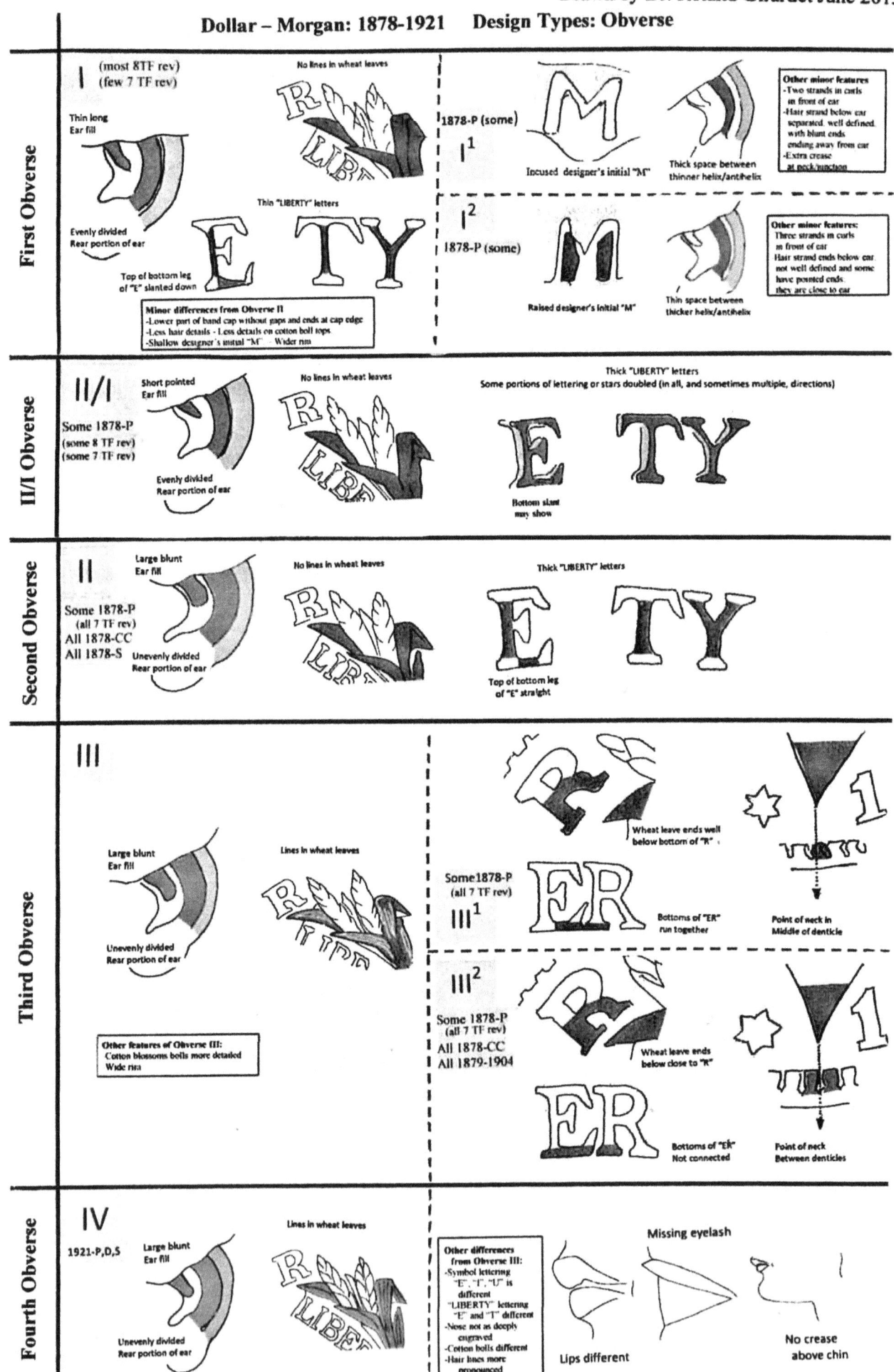

First Obverse

I (most 8TF rev) (few 7 TF rev)

No lines in wheat leaves

Thin long Ear fill

Evenly divided Rear portion of ear

Thin "LIBERTY" letters

Top of bottom leg of "E" slanted down

Minor differences from Obverse II
-Lower part of band cap without gaps and ends at cap edge
-Less hair details - Less details on cotton boll tops
-Shallow designer's initial "M"   Wider rim

I^1 1878-P (some)

Incused designer's initial "M"

Thick space between thinner helix/antihelix

Other minor features
-Two strands in curls in front of ear
-Hair strand below ear separated, well defined, with blunt ends ending away from ear
-Extra crease at neck/junction

I^2 1878-P (some)

Raised designer's initial "M"

Thin space between thicker helix/antihelix

Other minor features:
Three strands in curls in front of ear
Hair strand ends below ear not well defined and some have pointed ends, they are close to ear

II/I Obverse

II/I

Some 1878-P (some 8 TF rev) (some 7 TF rev)

Short pointed Ear fill

Evenly divided Rear portion of ear

No lines in wheat leaves

Thick "LIBERTY" letters
Some portions of lettering or stars doubled (in all, and sometimes multiple, directions)

Bottom slant may show

Second Obverse

II

Some 1878-P (all 7 TF rev) All 1878-CC All 1878-S

Large blunt Ear fill

Unevenly divided Rear portion of ear

No lines in wheat leaves

Thick "LIBERTY" letters

Top of bottom leg of "E" straight

Third Obverse

III

Large blunt Ear fill

Unevenly divided Rear portion of ear

Lines in wheat leaves

Other features of Obverse III:
Cotton blossoms bolls more detailed
Wide rim

III^1 Some 1878-P (all 7 TF rev)

Wheat leave ends well below bottom of "R"

Bottoms of "ER" run together

Point of neck in Middle of denticle

III^2 Some 1878-P (all 7 TF rev) All 1878-CC All 1879-1904

Wheat leave ends below close to "R"

Bottoms of "ER" Not connected

Point of neck Between denticles

Fourth Obverse

IV

1921-P,D,S

Large blunt Ear fill

Unevenly divided Rear portion of ear

Lines in wheat leaves

Other differences from Obverse III:
-Symbol lettering "E", "T", "U" is different "LIBERTY" lettering "E" and "T" different
-Nose not as deeply engraved
-Cotton bolls different
-Hair lines more pronounced

Missing eyelash

Lips different

No crease above chin

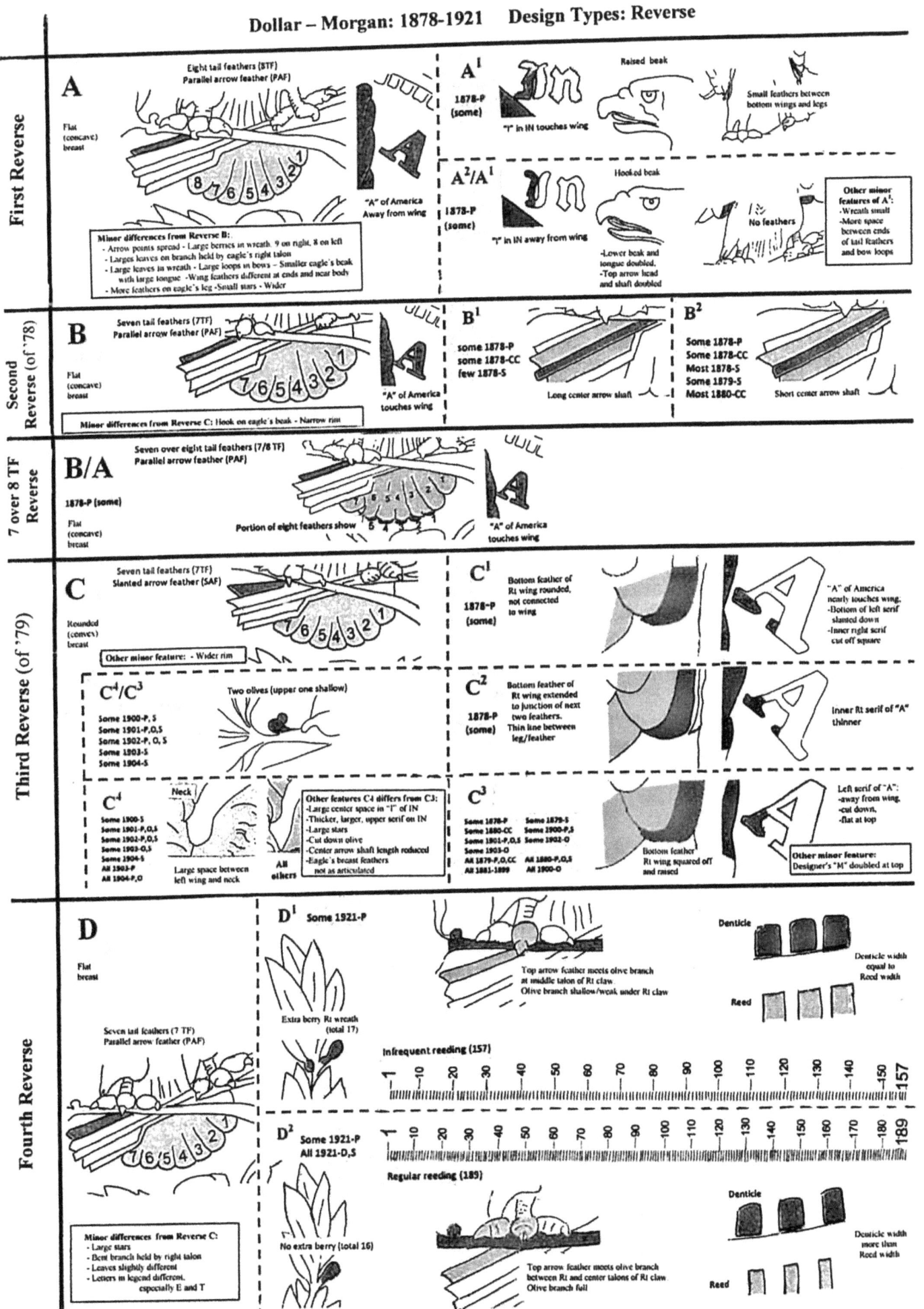

DIE VARIETIES

Differences from the normal design on working dies that struck coins can be categorized as **die varieties** that are either **unintentional** or **intentional modifications** of their design or changes due to **normal wear** from usage. **Unintentional** or **accidental** flaws appeared on the dies during their preparation or later during their use. Examples are the doubling of the design, date digits, mint mark, date and mint mark positions outside the normal range, gouges and scratches and over polished dies. **Intentional modifications** to the dies as they were prepared include overdates, over mint marks, identifying marks and dashes below the date digits, misplaced date digits to test die hardness, dual hubbing, design changes, die repair or touch-up engraving.

Dies were normally used until they **wore out** from the cracks, breaks and excessive wear of roughness and chips. These flaws in the dies can also be considered as die varieties and they weren't specifically created but occurred randomly, mainly late in the die's lifetime.

The category of die varieties include many thousands of listing for the thousands of Morgan working dies. It is the **main focus of this book** and includes many fascinating and unique die changes, such as crude dual hubbing of the 1878 P 7 over 8 tail feathers die varieties, touch up engraving on many 1878 and 1879 dies, use of acid treatment on some 1878 S, 1879 S and 1882 S dies and the touch up engraving of most of the 1921 P, D and S working dies.

ACCIDENTAL DIE FLAWS

This category of die varieties includes many different types of flaws on working dies that happened accidentally or unintentionally. An obvious type of flaw are the gouges and scratches on working dies and the Morgan dollar has some spectacular ones such as the **1890 CC Tail Bar** and **1878 S gouge** across the Liberty head Phrygian cap. Other popular die variety categories are the doubled date, mint mark and design. Here again, there are some spectacular ones such as the **1888 O** doubled Liberty head or **Hot Lips, 1887 O shifted date** and **1895 S shifted mint mark**. Some dies have a wrong size mint mark such as the **1903 micro S**. Even the mint mark and date digits have examples of their being punched far from the normal location and upright position. Other dies have strange impressions on them such as threads during the hubbing operation or edges of denticles when the dies were installed in the coining presses and accidentally bumped against each other. Even the edge reeding wasn't immune to flaws as many New Orleans coins show overlapping reeding collar flaws.

Date Digit Doubling

Die doubling on the date digits is the **most common listed die variety** for the Morgan dollar series. Some or all of the date digits were punched into about 3,500 obverse working dies **by hand** from 1879 thru 1904. It would take several hammer taps on a single digit or multiple taps on a 2-4 digit logotype to impress the date digits into the softened working die before they were finally hardened. All of the working dies were produced at the Philadelphia Mint and the date digits and mint marks were punched into the dies there.

For **1878 and 1921**, the **complete date** was in the master die and working hubs and there was no variation in their digit designs and placement for those two years. Any doubling on the date digits for those two years occurred usually with doubling on the adjacent design due to mis-alignment between the hub blows. There are a couple cases of 1878 working dies having doubling on one or two digits that may have been strengthened with single digit punches because of flaws in hastily prepared first design 8 tail feathers dies.

For **1879**, the right 8 was ground off the master hub **leaving 187.** The 9 was punched individually into working dies, or a two or four digit logotype was used to add the 9 to keep the digit spacing consistent. This resulted in die doubling of only the 9, 79 or all four digits from mis-alignment between digit blows. For **1880 thru 1883**, two right digits were removed from the master hub **leaving 18.** Again, single punches or two or four digit logotypes were used to punch in the date that also resulted in digit doubling on one, two, three or four digits. There was also no date placement variation for the years 1879- 1883, but often the right two digits were at different heights or thickness on the coin than the left two digits.

The **master hub** in 1884 had **all date digits removed** and the **entire date** with **slightly smaller digits** was punched into the working dies from **1884 thru 1904.** The use of two and four digit logotypes plus occasional single digit punch resulted in more even date digit heights or thickness, but the date positions varied. See the separate section on **Date Position Variations**. The **doubling has to be clearly visible with a 7X or 10X hand glass to be listed as a die variety.**

There are many hundreds of Morgan dollar die varieties with doubled date digits. Some examples are shown in the accompanying photographs. One of the largest shifts of date digit punching is the well-known **1887 O VAM 2** with underlying punch showing as a large shift of doubling at the 1 top and 7 left side plus additional doubling at the 7 top. The **1898 O VAM 20** has curved remains of digits between the 8 and 9 and 9 and 8 and this large digit shift variety is quite rare. The **1886 P VAM 20** has widely spaced doubling at the bottom of the 1 and inside the lower loop of the 6. A large shift upwards shows on the underlying digits of the **1891 O VAM 20**. Another dramatic shift upwards of the under lying 8 & 6 digits is the **1896 O VAM 19**. There are an **amazing number** and variations of digit doubling to be seen on the Morgan dollars just using a 7X of 10X hand glass.

The **VAM number** refers to a specific die variety listing in the **VAM book** mentioned in the **Introduction** and subsequent yearly **VAM Supplements**.

Available references–
Comprehensive Catalog and Encyclopedia of Morgan & Peace Dollars, by Leroy C Van Allen & A. George Mallis, 4th ed., 1998, WorldWide Ventures.
1878 Morgan Dollar 8-TF Attribution Guide, by Jeff Oxman & Les Hartnett, 3rd ed., 2004.
A Guide to the Varieties of the 1878 Carson City Morgan Dollar, by John Roberts, 2010.
1878 P 7 Tail Feathers Morgan Dollar Attribution Guide, by Leroy Van Allen, Revised November 2010.
1878 S Morgan Dollar Attribution Guide, by Leroy Van Allen & Craig Lickenbrock, Updated March 2009.
1902 O Morgan Dollar Series Attribution Guide, by Alan Scott, 2010.
1904 O Morgan Dollar Series Attribution Guide, by Alan Scott, 2010.
Top 100 Morgan Dollar Varieties: The VAM Keys, by Michael Fey & Jeff Oxman, 4th ed., 2009.
SSDC Official Guide to the Hot 50 Morgan Dollar Varieties, by Jeff Oxman, 2000.
Official Guide to the Morgan Dollar Hit List 40, by Jeff Oxman, 2009.

1887 O VAM 1 Doubled 1

1887 O VAM 2 Tripled 7

1898 O VAM 20 Re-punched Date

1886 P VAM 20 Doubled Date

1891 O VAM 20 Shifted Date

1896 O VAM 19 Shifted Date

1878 P VAM 170 Doubled Date

1879 P VAM 36 Doubled Date

1878 CC VAM 13 Doubled Date

1879 P VAM 59 Doubled 879

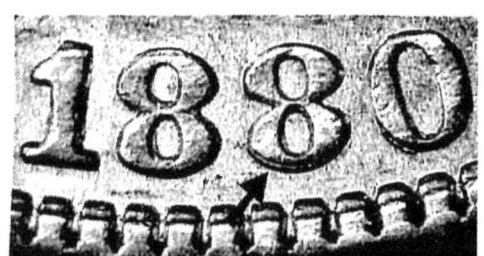

1880 P VAM 22 Doubled Date

1880 S VAM 7 Doubled Date

1884 CC VAM 7 Doubled 18

1883 P VAM 4 Doubled 1-83

1883 CC VAM 4 Doubled Date

1885 P VAM 6 Doubled Date

1886 P VAM 5 Doubled 18

1886 Proof VAM 15 Doubled 18-6,
Dash Under 8

1887 P VAM 5 Doubled 887

1889 P VAM 6 Doubled 1

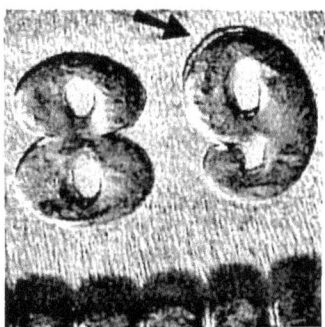

1889 P VAM 6 Doubled 9

1889 O VAM 6 Doubled 18

1889 O VAM 6 Doubled 9

1890 P VAM 4 Doubled 1-90

1890 CC VAM 3 Doubled 90

1890 S VAM 12 Doubled 1-90

1896 P VAM 20 Bar 6 Over 6

1896 P VAM 3 Doubled 89

1900 O VAM 39 Doubled/Tripled 0s

Date Position Variations

Because the two or more date digits were in the master hub from 1878 thru 1883, the date position and orientation didn't vary for those years. In **1878** the **entire date** was in the master hub. For **1879**, the right 8 was ground off the master hub and the **9** was punched individually into working dies or a two or four digit logotype was used to add the 9 into the working dies. Any shift of the four digit logo type between blows would create doubling on some of the digits.

For the years **1880 thru 1883, both right digits** were removed from the master hub. If a four digit logotype was used, then often the left two digits ended up deeper in the die from being entered more often than the right two digits. This resulted in the coins having higher 18 than the right two digits and an **uneven** looking date **thickness**.

Beginning in **1884**, the master hub had all **date digits removed** and the date digits were made slightly **smaller**. All the date digits were punched by hand into each working die using a single digit punch or two or four digit logotype. This resulted in more even date digit thickness on the coins but the date lateral position and orientations varied from **1884 thru 1904**. The **complete date** was in the master hub again for **1921** and all the date positions and orientation are the same for this year.

Five nominal date **lateral positions** are used to describe the date positions from 1884 thru 1904. The **left edge** of the lower crossbar of the **1** is used as an **index**. Normal range falls within the top of the **third denticle** from the Liberty head neck vee point. The space between the denticles on either side of this third denticle is defined as **near** and **far date** position. Beyond this left and right denticle space is defined as **very near** and **very far**.

Most date positions from 1884 thru 1904 fall within the normal lateral position with the left side of the 1 base over the third denticle from the Liberty head neck point. Curiously, few dates from 1884 thru 1886 have the near and very near positions whereas quite a few fall outside the normal range into the far and very far designations. Beyond 1886 there are quite a number of near and far dates and a few very near and very far dates. In addition, there are some date vertical positions of **low** and **high** plus **slanted** for many of these years because of the hand punching of the date digits into the working dies.

However, the date lateral and vertical orientation positions doesn't affect the variety premium price, but is useful to identify specific die varieties. Some examples of date position variations are shown in the accompanying photographs.

1880 P VAM 38 Doubled 80, Low 0

1890 O VAM 7 Slanted Date

1891 P VAM 11 Far High Date

1896 P VAM 4 Low Near Date

1895 O VAM 5 Low Far Date

1888 P Near Slanted Date

1889 P Far Date, High 9

1900 O Very Near Date

1889 P Very Far Date

Mint Mark Doubling

Slight doubling of the Morgan dollar mint mark is not unusual because they were punched by hand into the about 2,500 branch mint reverse dies. The 1878 CC & S mint marks and the 1921 D & S mint marks were **very small** in size and rarely had any significant doubling on them. This was likely due to fewer hammer blows needed to punch the mint marks into the reverse die. However the small size of the 1878 CC & S mint marks **tended to fill up**, so **larger** size mint marks were used from 1879 thru 1904, except for a couple isolated cases in 1879, 1880 and 1903.

All branch mint Morgan dollars working reverse dies had the mint mark punched in **by hand** at the Philadelphia Mint. They were punched into the dies after they had been annealed following the design hubbing sequences, but before the dies were polished and hardened. No information is available on the contemporary process of punching the mint marks into the reveres dies. However, the author witnessed the punching of the mint marks into an Eisenhower die at the Philadelphia Mint in 1978 which would have been similar for the Morgan dollar dies. Each die was clamped into a vise and the mint mark punch carefully lowered against the die face and lined up in position by eye. Three quick taps within less than a second were then given to the punch by a hammer. A quick visual inspection with the naked eye was given to the mint mark to determine if it was deep enough with proper placement and orientation. Either sketches or specimen pieces would have been used to show the preferred mint mark position.

One of the most dramatic examples of mint mark doubling is the **1895 S VAM 4** with a mis-positioned first S mint mark punched in **sideways** under the normal S mint mark. A serif of the bottom of an S shows at the top left outside of the normal S mint mark. A very **large shift** of a S mint mark punch is the **1895 S VAM 3** with the underlying S shifted way up to the top left. Another dramatic example of mis-positioned mint mark is the **1879 O VAM 4** that has the horizontal bars of a **sideways** O mint mark within the normal O mint mark. Other examples of mint mark doubling include some significant doubling of the **CC mint mark** as shown for the 1884 CC VAM 5, 1890 CC VAM 5 and 1892 CC VAM 4. Dramatic doubling on the **O mint mark** occurs for the 1882 O VAM 7, 1883 O VAM 4, 1884 O VAM 6, 1886 O VAM 7, 1888 O VAM 15 and 1902 O VAM 8. The 1881 O VAM 5 has a doubled O mint mark on the right inside with a die gouge at the top let inside making it resemble slightly the 1882 O/S over mint mark series. Some strong doubling on the **S mint mark** examples are the 1879 S VAM 30, 1880 S VAM 18, 1881 S VAM 5, 1885 S VAM 6, 1887 S VAM 2, 1890 VAMs 2 & 3. Two very large shifts of the S mint mark doubling occurred for the 1896 S VAM 5 and the 1898 S VAM 6.

Available references—

A Guide to the Varieties of the 1878 Carson City Morgan Dollar, by John Roberts, 2010.

1878 S Morgan Dollar Attribution Guide, by Leroy Van Allen & Craig Lickenbrock, Updated March 2009.

1902 O Morgan Dollar Series Attribution Guide, by Alan Scott, 2010.

1904 O Morgan Dollar Series Attribution Guide, by Alan Scott, 2010.

Top 100 Morgan Dollar Varieties: The VAM Keys, by Michael Fey & Jeff Oxman, 4th ed., 2009.

SSDC Official Guide to the Hot 50 Morgan Dollar Varieties, by Jeff Oxman, 2000.

Official Guide to the Morgan Dollar Hit List 40, by Jeff Oxman, 2009.

Punching Mint Mark Into Die, 1970s

Mint Mark Punches & Specimens, 1970s

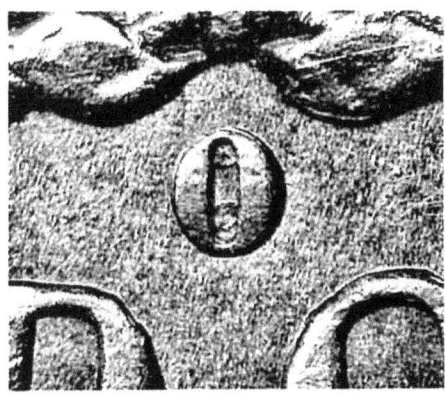

1879 O VAM 4 O/O Horizontal

1895 S VAM 3 S/S

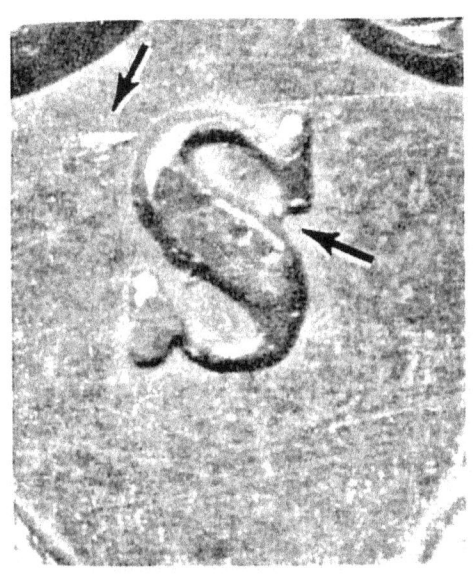

1895 S VAM 4 S Over Horizontal S   .

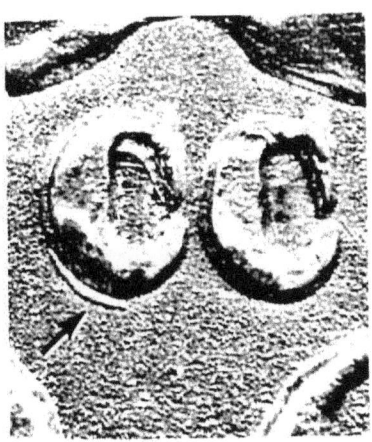

1884 CC VAM 5 Doubled CC

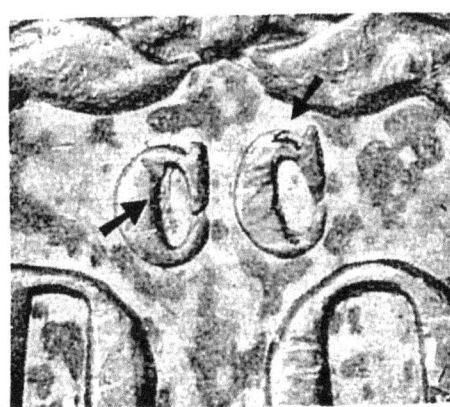

1890 CC VAM 5 Doubled CC

1892 CC VAM 4 CC Over CC Down

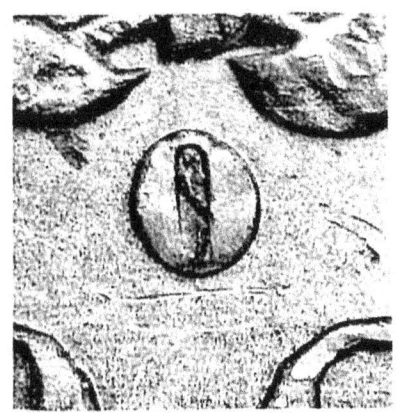

1881 O VAM 5 O/O Rt. Inside

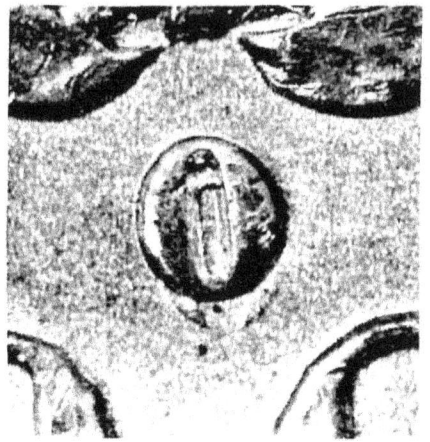

1882 O VAM 7 O Over O Low

1883 O VAM 4 O/O Low

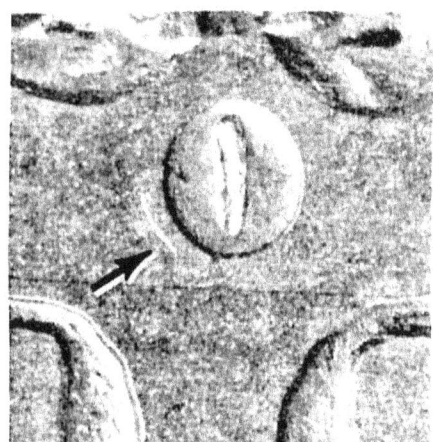

1884 O VAM 6 O Over O Left & Down

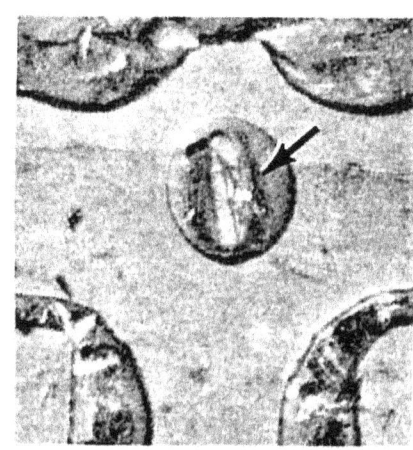

1884 O VAM 7 O Over O Tilted Left

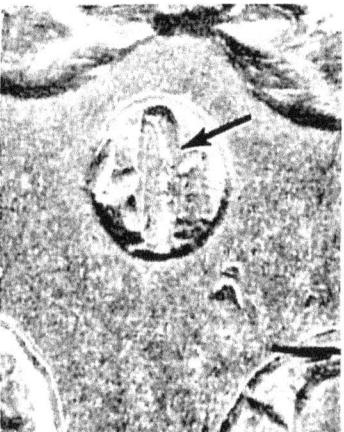

1884 O VAM 9 O Over O Right

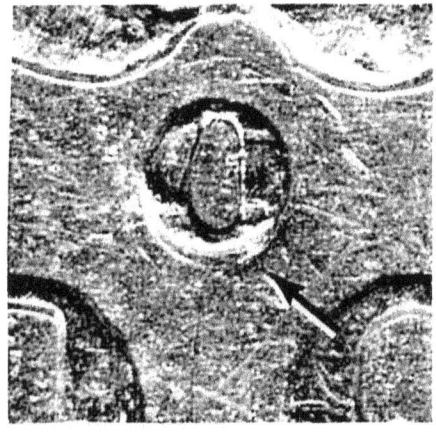

1886 O VAM 7 O Over O Down

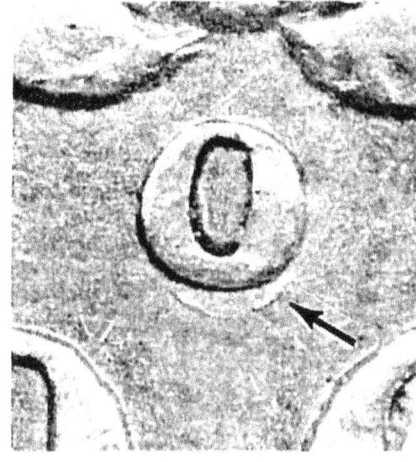

1888 O VAM 15 O Over O Low

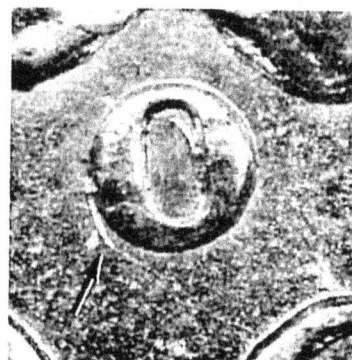

1902 O VAM 8 O Over O Down

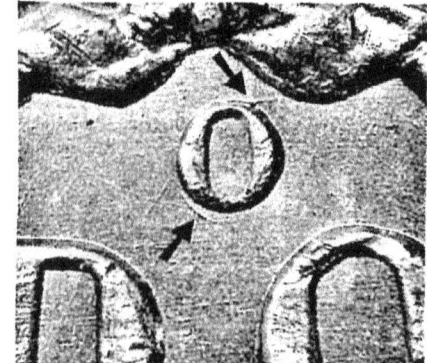

1903 O VAM 12 O/O Down

1879 S VAM 30 S Over S

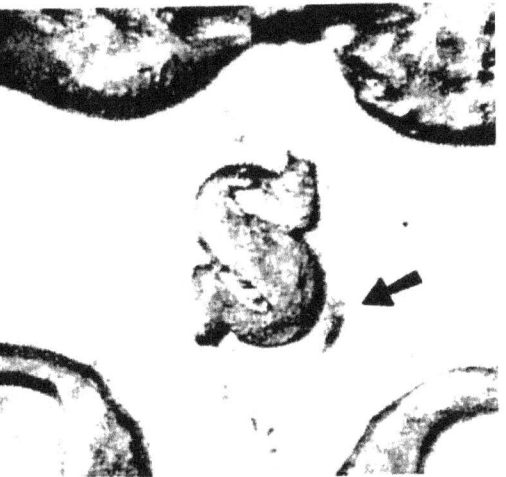

1879 S VAM 49 S Over S Far Right

1880 S VAM 19 S Over S Tripled

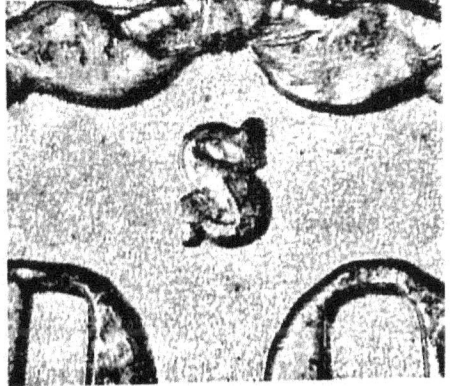

1881 S VAM 5 S/S Left

1885 S VAM 6 S Over S Left

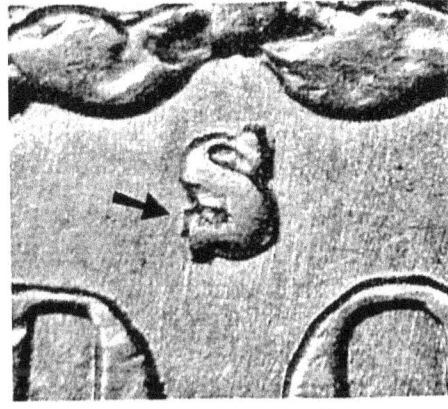

1886 S VAM 2 S/S

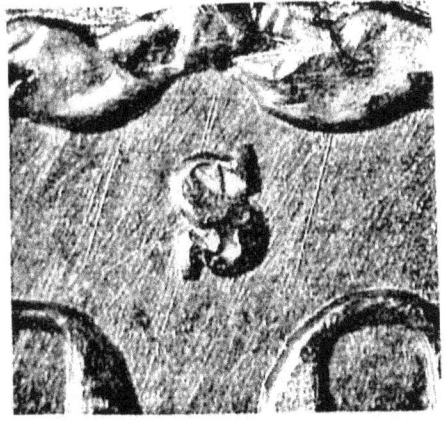

1887 S VAM 2 S/S Left

1890 S VAM 3 S/S Down

1896 S VAM 5 S Over S Right & Up

1898 S VAM 6 S Over S Down

-33-

Mint Mark Position Variations

The normal mint mark position was in the area below the wreath bow and above the tops of DO in DOLLAR. Because the mint marks were punched into the working dies **by hand** at the Philadelphia Mint, there was variation in the **height, lateral** position and **tilt**. This resulted in quite a few examples of the mint mark being positioned outside the normal range.

Normal height and lateral tolerance was selected to incorporate most mint mark positions found on the coins. This was a **box** roughly with the **top even with the bottom of the wreath ribbon, bottom even with the top of DO** and **left** and **right** sides **even with the right inside of D** and **left inside of the O.** The tilt tolerance is more subjective and applies visually when the mint mark **looks obviously tilted** from the normal vertical thru the coin middle.

There are hundreds of listed Morgan dollar varieties that have mint mark positioned outside of the normal range. Most are a little outside this range, but some are quite spectacular in their tilt or position shift. A few examples are shown in the accompanying photographs.

1878 CC VAM 2 CC Shifted Left

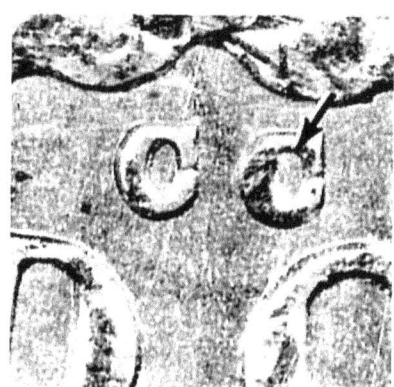
1878 CC VAM 15 CC Shifted Right

1878 CC VAM 3 C Set High & Right

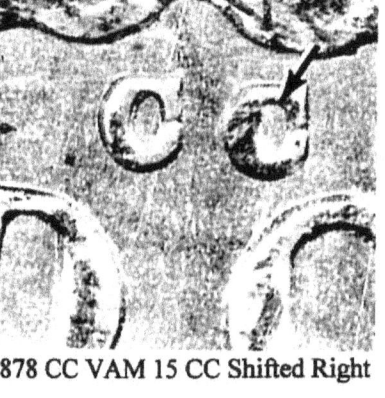
1878 CC VAM 16 Wide CC Set Right & High

1878 CC VAM 30 Close CC

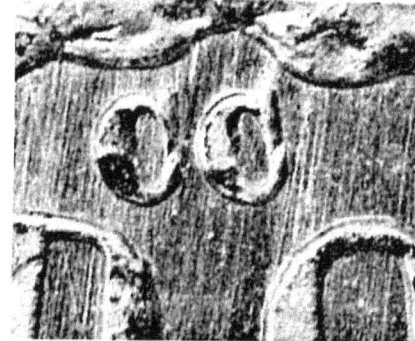
1879 CC VAM 2 CC Tilted Left

1879 CC VAM 4 CC Shifted Left

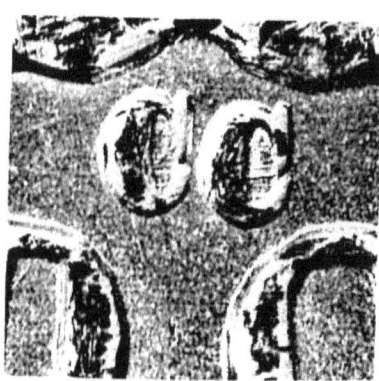
1883 CC VAM 2 Close CC

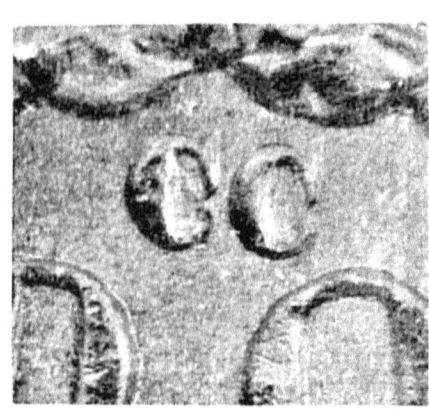
1883 CC VAM 8 CC Shifted Right

1885 CC VAM 3 CC Tilted Left

1889 CC VAM 5 Dropped C

1890 CC VAM 3 CC Tilted Left

1892 CC VAM 10 Wide CC

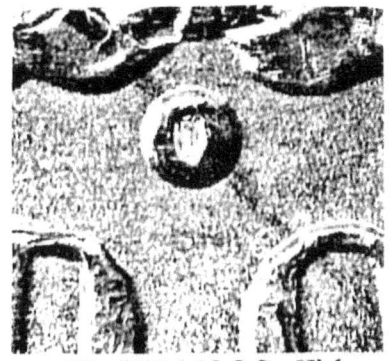

1880 O VAM 8 O Set High

1880 O VAM 25 O Shifted Right

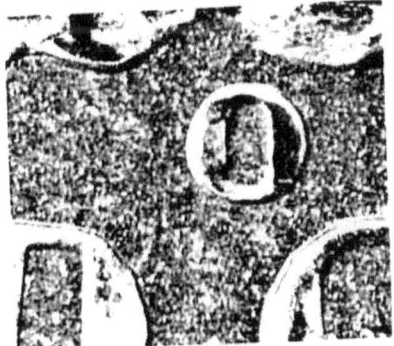

1885 O VAM 8 O Shifted Right

1888 O VAM 8 Very High O Set Right

1889 O VAM 9 O Set High

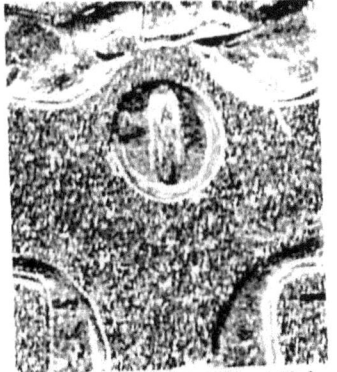

1889 O VAM 17 O Set High

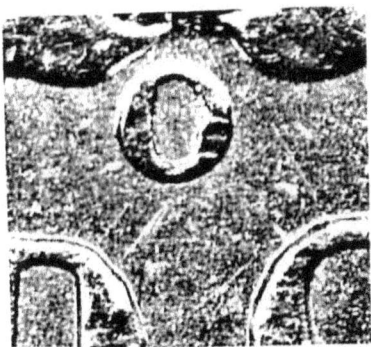

1897 O VAM 5 High O Set Left

1897 O VAM 9 High O Tilted Right

1900 O VAM 15 O Set High & Left

1903 O VAM 3 O Tilted Left

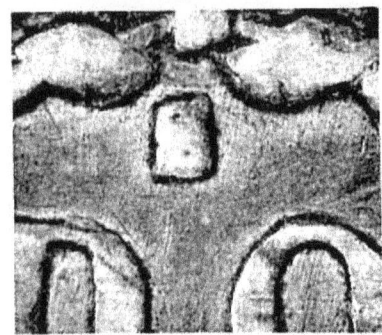

1878 S VAM 77 S Set High

1879 S VAM 33 S Shifted Right

1880 S VAM 3 S Tilted Left

1880 S VAM 84 S Tilted Very Far Left

1881 S VAM 22 S Shifted Left

1882 S VAM 20 S Tilted Far Left

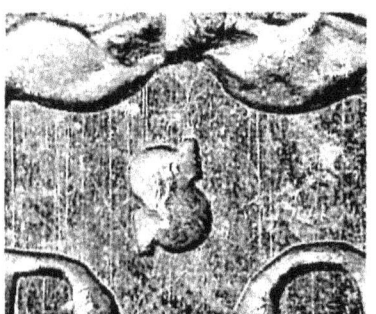

1882 S VAM 29 S Tilted Left

1882 S VAM 30 S Set Right & Low, Tilted Left

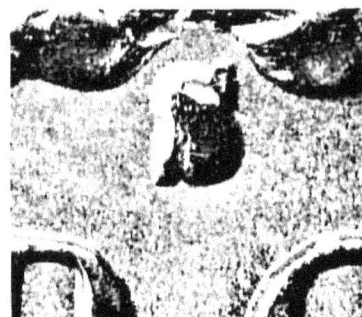

1890 S VAM 9 S Set High

1890 S VAM 17 S Tilted Left

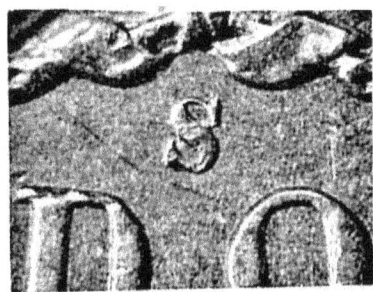

1895 S VAM 2 S Tilted Right

1899 S VAM 5 S Tilted Right

1921 D VAM 16 D Tilted Left

1921 D VAM 20 D Set Left, Tilted Left

1921 S VAM 2 S Shifted Left

Design Doubling

Design doubling can occur anywhere on the lettering, stars, date and Liberty head on the obverse and the lettering, wreaths, eagle and mint mark on the reverse. Doubling on the date digits, ears and profile are treated separately as well as the mint mark doubling on the reverse.

The doubling on the designs occurred during the **hubbing** of the **working dies** at the Philadelphia Mint. Each Morgan working die required seven to ten blows from the working hub to fully transfer the complete design across the die face. Early blows from the hub only transferred some of the central design. The working dies started out as a shallow cone and were increasingly flattened by each working hub blow until the full design was transferred out to the denticles.

Slight **mis-alignment** between the working hub and working die **during the hubbing blow** would result in doubling on the working die. Doubling only on the central part would be caused by mis-alignment during an early hub blow, whereas doubling at the central and/or outer portions would be from mis-alignment during later hub blows. Since some or all of the date digits and the mint marks were punched into the fully hubbed working die, their doubling would generally be in a **different** direction than any doubling on the design.

Working dies were usually inspected between each working hub blow, but numerous examples of die doubling exist with some quite pronounced for the Morgan dollar. The early 1878 P dies had many examples of die doubling because of the pressure to strike the Morgan dollars in the required quantities and the rush to perfect the design of the dies.

Die doubling can be identified from dual hub doubling discussed in a separate section. A **doubled die** will have a **progressive shift of the same design** while a **dual hub die** will have **different features of the two designs** visible at various places on the die.

The most prominent doubled obverse die is the **1888 O VAM 4** so-called **Hot Lips**. It has very pronounced separation of the lips and chin with the wheat leaves above LIBERTY strongly doubled to the right and much of the upper hair strands doubled. The doubling occurred at the middle stages of the die hubbing sequences. It commands a strong premium in all grades.

The most prominent doubled reverse die is the **1901 P VAM 4 Shifted Eagle**. A fairly early mis-alignment of a hubbing blow resulted in strongly doubled bottom of the eagle's tail feathers, wings and lower beak plus the olive branches and leaves, arrow shafts and arrow heads plus the letters od and W in the motto in God We Trust. It also commands a significant premium in all grades.

There are many doubled dies with doubling on stars, eyelid, letters, wreaths and other parts of the design for the Morgan dollar series. Some examples are shown in the accompanying photographs.

Available references–
1878 Morgan Dollar 8-TF Attribution Guide, by Jeff Oxman & Les Hartnett, 3rd ed., 2004.
A Guide to the Varieties of the 1878 Carson City Morgan Dollar, by John Roberts, 2010.
1878 P 7 Tail Feathers Morgan Dollar Attribution Guide, by Leroy Van Allen, Revised November 2010.
1878 S Morgan Dollar Attribution Guide, by Leroy Van Allen & Craig Lickenbrock, Updated March 2009.
1902 O Morgan Dollar Series Attribution Guide, by Alan Scott, 2010.
1904 O Morgan Dollar Series Attribution Guide, by Alan Scott, 2010.
Top 100 Morgan Dollar Varieties: The VAM Keys, by Michael Fey & Jeff Oxman, 4th ed., 2009.
SSDC Official Guide to the Hot 50 Morgan Dollar Varieties, by Jeff Oxman, 2000.
Official Guide to the Morgan Dollar Hit List 40, by Jeff Oxman, 2009.
Morgan Silver Dollars, by Q. David Bowers, Whitman Publishing, 2004.

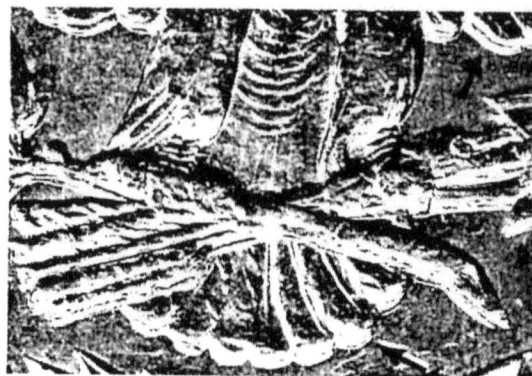

1901 P VAM 3 Shifted Eagle

888 O VAM 4 Doubled Lips & Eyelid 1888 O VAM 4 Doubled Hair & Cotton Leaves

1878 P VAM 5 Doubled Motto

1878 P VAM 8 Doubled Wing Feathers

1878 P VAM 7 Doubled Left Reverse

1878 P VAM 7 Tripled E

1878 P VAM 14-1 Alligator Eye & Spike

1878 P VAM 12 Doubled Stars

1878 P VAM 70 Doubled Motto Letters

-38-

1878 P VAM 187 Doubled R

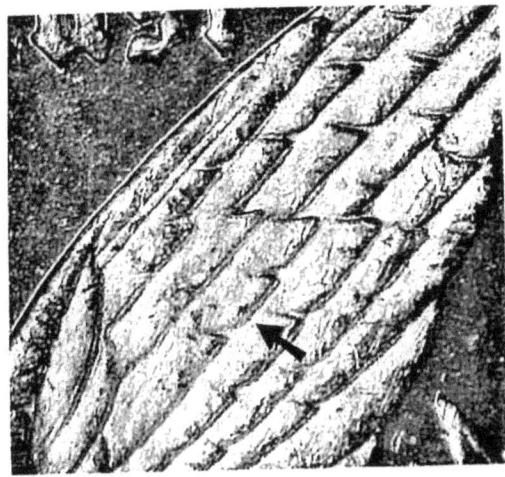

1878 P VAM 190 Doubled Wing Feathers

1878 CC VAM 6 Doubled Obverse

1878 S VAM 6 Doubled Motto

1878 S VAM 22 Doubled Motto RIB

1880 P VAM 44 Doubled Eyelid

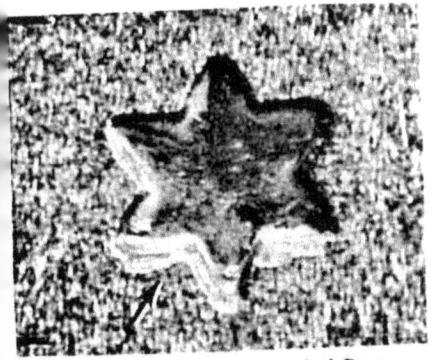

1883 P VAM 10 Sextupled Stars

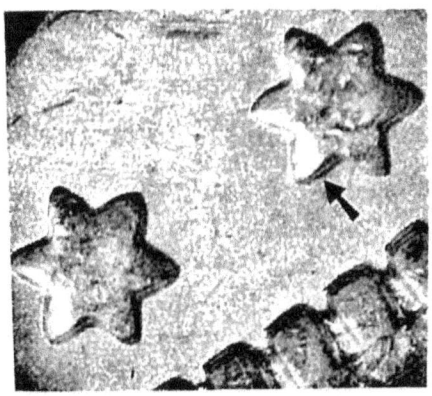

1883 O VAM 35 Doubled Right Stars

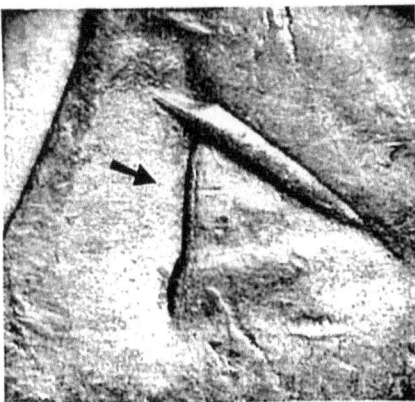

1885 P VAM 24 Alligator Eye

1887 O VAM 22A Doubled Eyelid

1887 S VAM 10 Doubled Legend

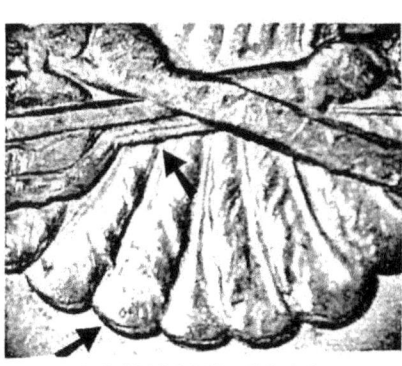

1888 O VAM 9 Doubled Arrows
& Tail Feathers

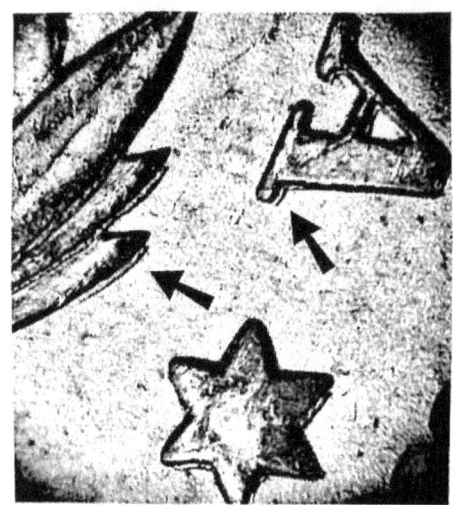

1888 O VAM 9 Doubled Wreath & Legend

1891 P VAM 10 Doubled Profile

1891 S VAM 3 Doubled Left Stars

1896 P VAM 4 Doubled Right Stars

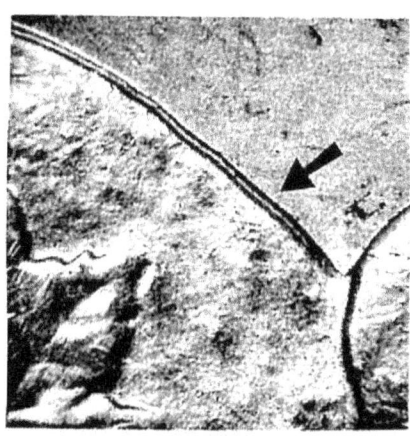

1897 P VAM 8 Doubled Cap Edge

1897 P VAM 8 Doubled Stars

1900 P VAM 11 Doubled Eagle

1900 O VAM 15 Doubled 2 Right Stars

1901 P VAM 17 Doubled Reverse

1901 O VAM 34 2 Eyelids

1902 O VAM 43 Tripled Eyelid Front

1902 O VAM 54 Doubled Eyelid

Doubled Ears

Doubling on the Morgan dollar Liberty head ear occurs on practically all of the years from 1878 thru 1904. It is most common for the years 1883 onward. One year, **1889 P**, has the most reported doubled ears which may be due to it's highest mintage of 21 million of the pre-1921 Morgan dollar and possibly their higher survival.

There are two causes of doubling of the ear: **hub doubling** and **die polishing doubling**. For **hub doubling**, the working die starts out as a cylinder with a shallow cone on one end. The working hubs were forced into the die cylinder face from **7 to 10 times** to transfer the entire design. Only a small part of the design was transferred with each hub blow and the die cylinder had to be annealed between each blow to soften the work hardened metal.

The ear on the Liberty head was in the center of the design and was the first part of the design to be transferred by the initial hub blow. **Registration** of the hub and die center design had to be made very carefully for the second and subsequent hub blows to avoid any doubling of the design. **Misalignment of the second or third hub blow** would cause doubling primarily on the **central design** that was the **ear** and little else. This hub doubling was the cause of doubling of the ear on the inside plus the outside and hair edge above the ear. If there is extensive doubling of the center of the Liberty head design, it usually includes a doubled ear. But most often doubling of just the ear and hair above the ear occurs. Strongly hub doubled ears occurred on the 1888 P, 1889 P, 1890 O, 1891 P, 1892 O, 1902 P and 1902 O and some of these can command premium prices.

The second cause of doubled ears is the much more common **die polishing**. The left inside and right inside and outside plus bottom earlobe edge were **high points** of a die design. **All pre-1921** Morgan **dies** were **basined** by a revolving disc to give slight curvature to the die face that allowed even fill across the die face as the coin was struck. A final die face polishing and buffing produced a mirror finish on the Morgan dollar die fields. This **final die polishing and buffing** was likely the **cause** of **rounding** of the die **high ear edges**. There are many listings of slightly doubled ear inside and earlobe bottom thru-out the Morgan dollar series. Most are minor doubling and don't command a premium.

The accompanying photographs show some examples of the hub doubled ears and die polishing doubling.

Available references–
1889 P Doubled Ear Morgan Dollar Attribution Guide, by Leroy Van Allen, Revised June 2009.
1902 O Morgan Dollar Series Attribution Guide, by Alan Scott, 2010.
Top 100 Morgan Dollar Varieties: The VAM Keys, by Michael Fey & Jeff Oxman, 4th ed., 2009.
SSDC Official Guide to the Hot 50 Morgan Dollar Varieties, by Jeff Oxman, 2000.
Official Guide to the Morgan Dollar Hit List 40, by Jeff Oxman, 2009.

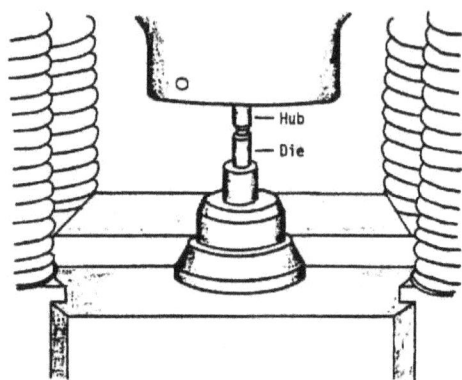

Second Hubbing Blow Set-up

Polished & Un-polished Ike Die Blanks, 1970s

1878 S VAM 86 Doubled Ear

1885 P VAM 1G Doubled Ear

1885 P VAM 27 Tripled Ear Bottom

1888 P VAM 11 Doubled Ear

1889 P VAM 16 Doubled Ear

1889 P VAM 42 Doubled Ear

1889 P VAM 20 Doubled Ear

1891 P VAM 2 Doubled Ear

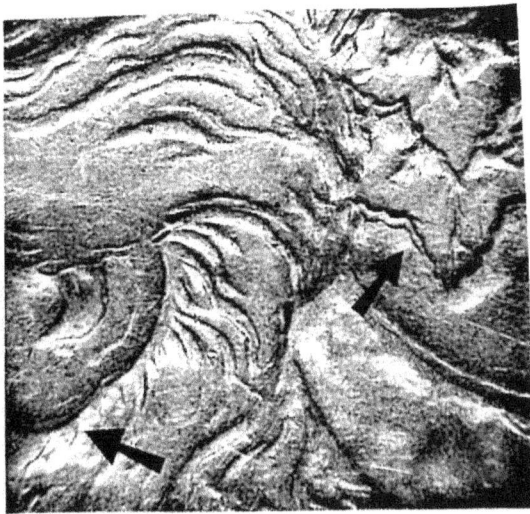

1890 O VAM 20 Doubled Ear & Cotton Leaves

1892 O VAM 5 Doubled Ear

1901 S VAM 10 Doubled Ear

1902 P VAM 4 Doubled Ear

1902 P VAM 18 Doubled Ear

1902 O VAM 25 Doubled Ear

1902 O VAM 43 Doubled Ear

1902 O VAM 54 Doubled Ear

Hub Doubling

There are a number of features on the Morgan dollar coins that has the same doubling flaws over many year and mints. These doubling are in the **master hub or die** and show up on **many** working hubs and **hundreds** of **working dies**. Other hub doubling may only show on a **few working dies** over a couple of years and would be in a **single working hub**.

Master Hub or Die Doubling

II obverse design type used in **1878** has slight doubling on the **right side of the 7** in the date.

III² obverse design type used from **1878 thru 1904** has a doubled **diagonal crossbar on N** in UNUM.

IV obverse design type used in **1921** has doubled **top of both 1's** in the date.

B reverse design type used in **1878 thru 1880** have slight doubling of the **3 & 4 tail feather ends**.

C⁴ reverse design type used from **1900 thru 1904** has doubling on the **left side of OLLA** in DOLLAR, bottom crossbar of the second A in AMERICA and slightly at bottom of U, E, D in UNITED and F in OF.

Working Hub Doubling

Doubling on a working hub will show up on several hundred working dies over a few years.

A **reverse working hub** of 1878 of the **C³ type** has **doubling** at the bottom inside of **UNITED STATES** letters, I of In at top, top right edge of eagle's right wing and left edge of some leaves in the left wreath. The **key identification** of this hub doubling is the strong doubling at the left inside of the **U in UNITED**. This hub doubling occurs on a few **1878 P 7TF reverse of 79** dies and some **1879 P, O & S** working dies.

Another **reverse working hub of 1878** of the **C³ type** has doubling on the outside edges of some **leaves in the left and right wreaths, tops of the serifs of A** next to the star in AMERICA, inside of AR in DOLLAR and right star towards the rim. The **doubling on the A** is the **key identifier** but can be weak or disappears when the die is excessively polished. This hub doubling occurs on a few **1878 P 7TF reverse of 79** working dies and some **1879 P, O and 1880 P** working dies.

A late date case of **reverse working hub** doubling occurs for some of the **1901 thru 1904 C⁴ type reverse** dies. It shows up as doubling on **UNITED STATES OF AMERICA,** upper right and left wreaths, In God We Trust and top of eagle's head. The **key identifiers** are the **tripled lower serif of N in UNITED** and doubled top of eagle's head.

Although interesting, master hub and die and working hub doubling usually doesn't carry any premium because they occur the same on so many working dies and coins. However, knowledge of them is useful so this type of doubling is not mistaken for working die doubling.

III² Hub Doubling N in UNUM

1878 S II Hub Doubled 7

1921 S IV Hub Doubling Top 1s

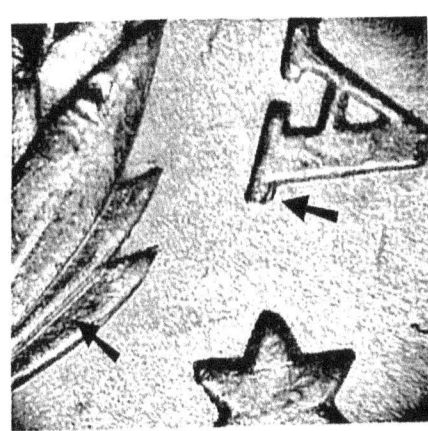

B Hub Doubling Tail Feather Ends

C³ Hub Doubling U

C³ Hub Doubling A Serif

C⁴ Hub Doubling A

C⁴ Hub Doubling U, Tripled N Serif

C⁴ Hub Doubling Top Eagle's Head

Counter Clash Doubling

Counter clash doubling is **doubling of the design features** in the **midst of die clash marks**. It most frequently occurred at the **Liberty head lips** and back of the **Phrygian cap near the ribbon**. Occasionally it shows up as doubled inside of the top of the **reverse left wreath** or **upper Liberty head neck**. The cause is the **slight shift of dies** between **two episodes of strong die clashing**. During the **first** clash episode the parts of the design of one die is transferred to the opposite die. The **second** strong clash episode with slight shift of the dies results in **some** of the initial transferred design to be **re-transferred** back to the original design with the **slight shift** causing the counter clash doubling.

It can be differentiated from normal die doubling of shifting between hub blows because of the limited area of length of the doubling and there is **always some strong die clash marks** around it. The counter clash doubling is fairly scarce because it requires two strong die clash episodes with a shift of dies between the two. But sometimes a strong clash of dies will slightly loosen a die in the coining press fixtures allowing the die rotation.

A strong counter clash doubled lips is the **1880 O VAM 50A**. The **1887 P VAM 1C** shows a counter clash at the cap back. A counter clash of the upper neck shows on the **1888 P VAM 9B**. The **1902 O VAM 26A** shows a counter clash at the right wreath leaf tips and at the upper neck.

Available references–
Elite Clashed Morgan Dollars, by Mark Kimpton, Sheriden Books, 2005.
Official Guide To The Hit List 40, by Jeff Oxman, 2009.

1879 O VAM 44A Counterclash Cap

1879 S VAM 66 Counterclash Lips

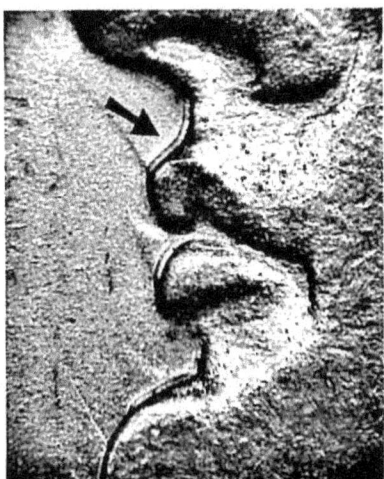

1880 P VAM 50A Doubled Lips
Counterclash

1882 CC VAM 2A Counterclash Lip

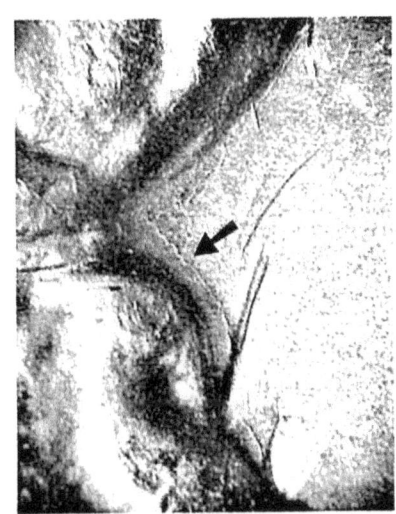

1882 CC VAM 3B Counterclash Cap

1882 CC VAM 3B Counterclash Lips

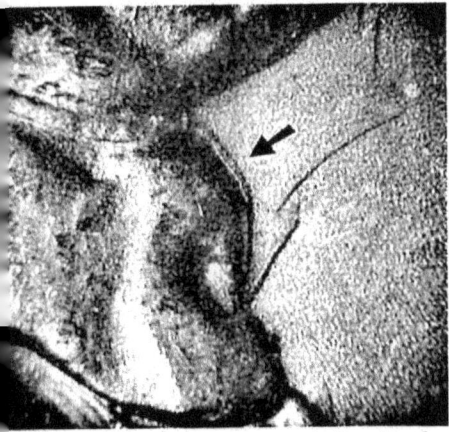

887 P VAM 1C Counterclash Cap Back

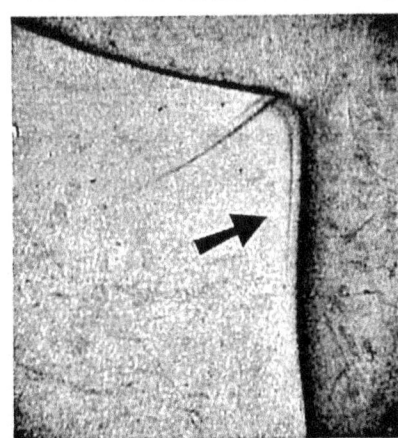

1888 P VAM 9B Counterclash Neck

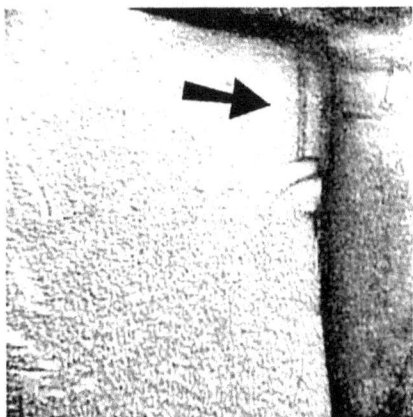

1902 O VAM 26A Double Clashed G,
Counterclash Neck

1904 O VAM 1B3 Counterclash Lips

1902 O VAM 26A Counterclash Leaf Tips

-47-

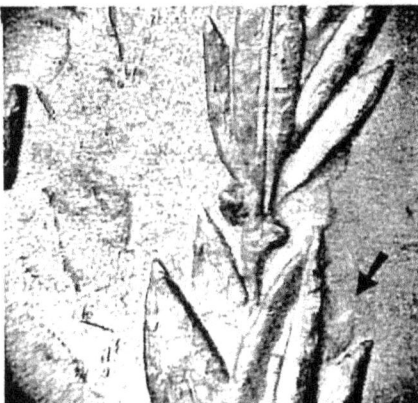

1904 O VAM 1B1 Counterclash
Wreath Leaf

Over Polished Dies

Over polished dies typically show **shallow design portions** and **letters** plus in extreme cases, **missing parts** of the design. The latter show up usually as **wide gaps and missing hair strands** at the Liberty head hair edge on the obverses. For the reverse, over polishing can result in **detached wreath leaves,** which is fairly common, and **missing portions of the feathers** in the **middle of the eagle's wings.**

Both the **first A and B type reverse designs used in 1878** had a similar over polishing problem of weakening or **removing the bottom inner feather next** to the **eagle's right leg.** Also, for the first **A type reverse,** over polishing did the same thing on the **inner feather** next to the **eagle's left leg.** The over polished **A type reverse** dies were all touched up by **engraving** small short 2-3 feathers at the left and right wing-leg junction as discussed in a separate section on **Engraved Eagle's Feathers.** The over polished **B type reverse dies** had **small touch up feathers** added to the eagle's right wing-leg junction and wing-body junction on some **1878 P dies.** Many **1878 S reverse dies** had a **full feather engraved** at the eagle's right wing-leg junction and some of these dies also had touch-up engraving in the middle of the wings and upper tail feathers.

The **C type reverse** used on some **1878 P** and from **1879 thru 1904** mainly had over polished die problems at the accompanying **III type obverse lower hair edge** and in the **reverse wreath leaves** and **middle** of the wings. These over polished areas on the reverse die were not touched up however.

There were special problems with the **1921 D type reverse dies** at all the mints with frequent **over polishing** at the **eagle's right leg** and **upper tail feathers,** plus the **middle** of the eagle's wings. All three 1921 P, D and S mints **added fine scribble lines** in these over polished areas on most reverse working dies in an attempt to fill in these over polished areas as discussed in the section on **1921 Scribbles.**

All the new Morgan dollar dies had the obverse and reverse die faces basined to give the proper curvature to strike-up the coins evenly. Some dies were later polished to remove die clash marks, gouges and cracks. This was performed on a revolving disc using coarse to fine grinding compounds. Very fine grit was used on a revolving disc to smooth the die fields to enable a mirror surface on the fields when buffed on the 1878 thru 1904 dies and on some 1921 dies. **Basining** and **polishing** of the **dies** was the **cause of over polished dies** that made design and lettering shallow across wide flat areas as opposed to buffing that caused field roughness and raised design edges on a coin.

An over polished and shallow L in LIBERTY is shown for the **1878 P 7 TF VAM 188.** The **1878 P VAM 116C** is a good example of the over polished and missing lower wing inner feathers. The **1878 P VAM 186B** has a severely over polished wing. The **1878 S VAM 48** has an over polished shallow ear and **1878 S VAM 17A** has over polished lower hair. A severely over polished eagle's head is the **1879 S VAM 50.** An example of over polished wreath bow is the **1879 S VAM 71.** Very shallow denticles is shown for the **1921 S VAM 5A.** Polishing bands at TAT in STATES occurred on the **1902 O VAM 26.** The over polished upper tail feathers and wing middle is pretty severe for the **1921 S VAM 28.** Another severely over polished upper tail feathers is the **1921 S VAM 1BV.**

Available references–
1878 P 7 Tail Feathers Morgan Dollar Attribution Guide, by Leroy Van Allen, Revised November 2010.
1878 S Morgan Dollar Attribution Guide, by Leroy Van Allen & Craig Lickenbrock, Updated March 2009.
1902 O Morgan Dollar Series Attribution Guide, by Alan Scott, 2010.
Official Guide to the Morgan Dollar Hit List 40, by Jeff Oxman, 2009.

878 P VAM 188/223 Washed Out L

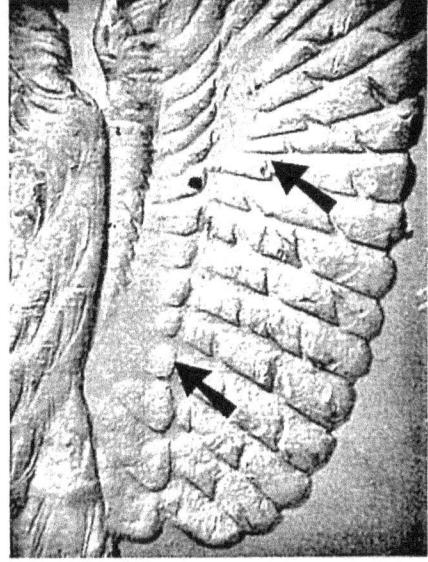

1878 P VAM 186 B Over Polished Wing

1878 S VAM 17A Over Polished Hair

1878 S VAM 106 Over Polished TED & Denticles

1878 S VAM 48 Over Polished Ear

1878 S VAM 101 Over Polished Wing Feathers

1878 P VAM 116C Polished Feather

1879 S VAM 16B Polished Tail Feathers

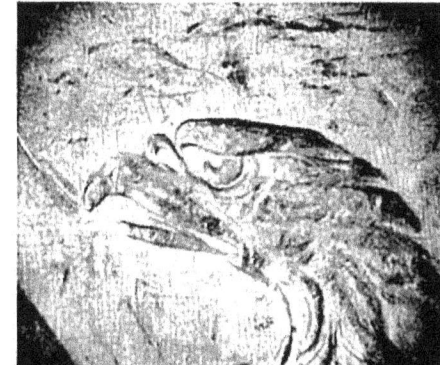

1879 S VAM 70 Over Polished Eagle's Head

1879 S VAM 71 Over Polished Wreath Bow

1879 S VAM 71 Over Polished Wreath Leaves

1879 S Over Polished Lower Reverse

1879 S VAM 75 Over Polished Reverse

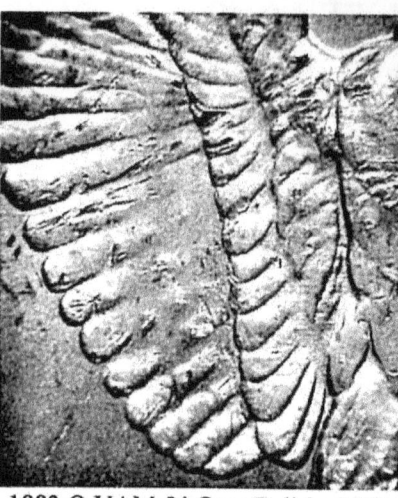

1883 O VAM 54 Over Polished Wing

1889 S VAM 6A Polished Arrow Heads

1902 O VAM 26 Polishing Bands

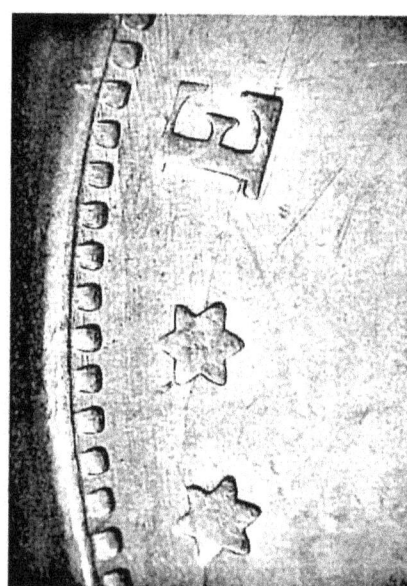

1921 S VAM 5A Shallow Denticles

1921 S VAM 1BV Over Polished Tail Feathers

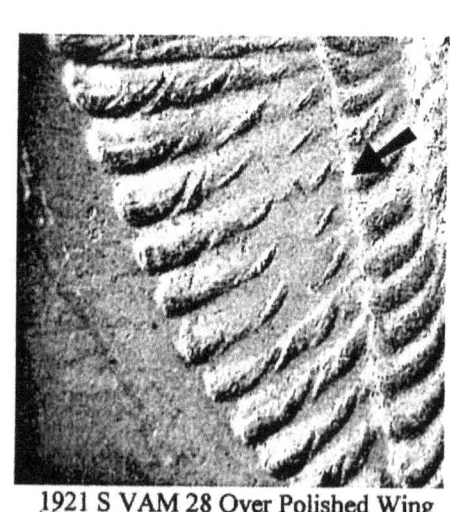

1921 S VAM 28 Over Polished Wing

1921 S VAM 28 Over Polished Wing

Over Buffed Dies

Over buffed dies occur when a **soft buffing wheel catches the edges** of portions of the design on a die face and **rounds them off.** Buffing of the Morgan dollar die face was performed to give the final **mirror-like surfaces** to the **fields.** Each mint performed the basining operations, polishing and buffing of the dies to match the requirements of the various coining presses at the mints. Buffing differs from die polishing that used fine polishing compounds on a slightly concave disc to give the die face the required curvature across the die face to evenly strike up the design on the coin. The die polishing also made the fields smooth so they could receive the final buffing for a mirror like finish.

There aren't very many known die varieties with obvious over buffed parts of the design or rims. The **1883 O** and **1891 S** each have an obvious **concave obverse die** with rounded periphery. This same **1883 O** variety also has a slightly **concave reverse die.** Sometimes there is only a portion of the field edge that is **beveled**, such as the **1891 S** below DOLLAR and below the eagle's tail feathers of an **1888 O.** Some coins show **raised edges of the wreath leaves or letters** when buffing rounded these parts of the design on a die. It differs from heavy die wear which has die chips and roughness. Examples shown in the accompanying photographs are the 1881 O, 1883 O, 1891 O and 1901 P. The **1883 O VAM 58** with buffed wreath is a pretty <u>extreme</u> example of over buffed die.

1878 S VAM 63 Beveled 8's

1881 O VAM 16 Polished Letters

1883 O VAM 1C Buffed Wreath

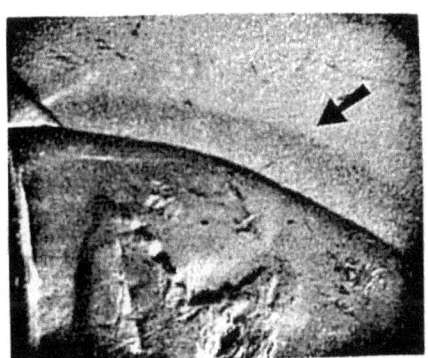

1883 O VAM 1H Beveled Field Cap Top

1883 O VAM 52 Concave Obverse

1883 O VAM 52 Concave Reverse
Rim

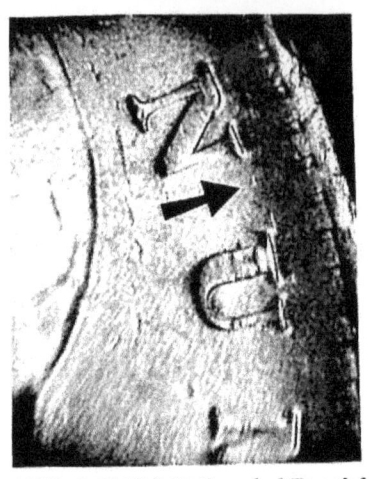

1883 O VAM 58 Beveled Denticles

1883 O VAM 58 Beveled Denticles

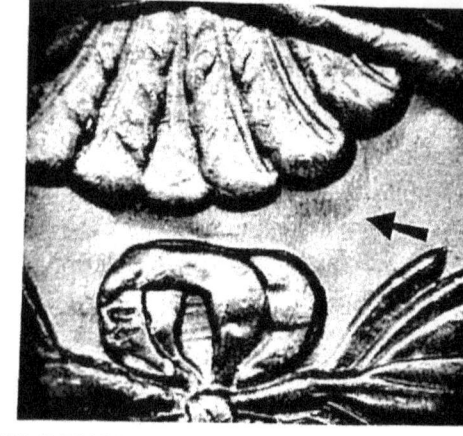

1888 O VAM 36A Bulge Below Tail Feathers

1891 O VAM 1D Over Buffed Reverse

1891 O VAM 19 Buffed Eagle

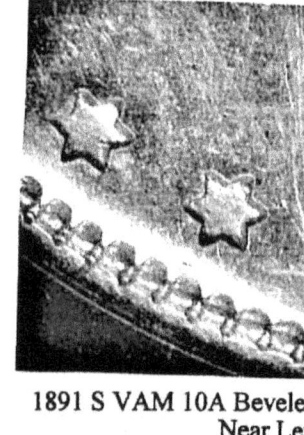

1891 S VAM 10A Beveled Field
Near Left Stars

1891 S VAM 10A Beveled Field
at DOLLAR

1891 S VAM 15 Concave Obverse

1891 O VAM 19 Buffed Wreath

1901 P VAM 20 Over Buffed Reverse

Die Gouges and Scratches

Out of over 7,000 Morgan dollar working dies made from 1878 thru 1904 plus perhaps 300 to 500 1921 working dies, many hundreds show die gouges and scratches. Only those readily **visible to the naked eye are listed as die varieties**. Tiny scratches and polishing lines not visible to the naked eye are on practically all Morgan dollar dies and are of little collector interest except sometimes as possible die markers to aid in identifying individual dies where needed.

Gouges and scratches can occur on working dies before they were first used in coining presses thru accidental damage **during transit** from the Philadelphia Mint where they were produced, at the mints as they were **moved around** and in the coining presses as they were **first being installed**. They can also occur during their lifetime of striking coins from the **contact of the feed fingers** that have malfunctioned and gotten out of position, **during the removal of dies** to repair and polish them or in **transit and storage** between multiple installations in coining presses as die pair were changed and mixed up.

One of the most prominent reverse die gouges is the so-called **1890 CC VAM 4 Tail Bar** with a wide gouge from the left tail feather down to the wreath leaves. It is one of the earliest die gouges reported in 1951. An **amazing** prominent series of die gouges on the obverse is the **1921 S VAM 1B Thorn Head** with seven sequences of die gouges followed by die polishing at the Phrygian cap and elsewhere that was reported in 1959. The **1888 P VAM 7** has five different die states of die gouges all over the reverse die and was reported in 1977. A couple of spectacular die gouges on the reverse of the **1882 CC VAM 2** late die state shows at O and LL in DOLLAR only recently reported in 2009. An early die state of this variety shows the top of a 1 below the left 8 that makes it double interesting!

The **longest and largest die gouge on the obverse die** is the **1878 S VAM 19** with a long and wide die gouge band from the wheat leaves thru the top cotton leaf over to the Phrygian cap fold that was reported in 1977. The **longest related series of die gouges in a line on the reverse** is the **1891 S VAM 1A/8A** with gouges in ends of olive branch leaves over to left adjacent wreath leaf and thru the upper part of the eagle's right leg that was reported in 1974. An unusual example of **die damage** is the **1881 O VAM 1D** with die flakes or gouges on the eye front. But the die with the **largest number of large die gouges, _by far_,** is the **1888 S VAM1A/13 Monster Gouges**, with over **30** large reverse die gouges in various directions all over the eagle that was reported in 1982.

Available references–
1878 Morgan Dollar 8-TF Attribution Guide, by Jeff Oxman & Les Hartnett, 3rd ed., 2004.
A Guide to the Varieties of the 1878 Carson City Morgan Dollar, by John Roberts, 2010
1878 P 7 Tail Feathers Morgan Dollar Attribution Guide, by Leroy Van Allen, Revised November 2010.
1878 S Morgan Dollar Attribution Guide, by Leroy Van Allen & Craig Lickenbrock, Updated March 2009.
1902 O Morgan Dollar Series Attribution Guide, by Alan Scott, 2010.
Amazing Changing 1921 S VAM 1B Thorn Head Morgan Dollar, by Leroy Van Allen, revised April 2011.
Top 100 Morgan Dollar Varieties: The VAM Keys, by Michael Fey & Jeff Oxman, 4th ed., 2009.
SSDC Official Guide to the Hot 50 Morgan Dollar Varieties, by Jeff Oxman, 2000.
Official Guide to the Morgan Dollar Hit List 40, by Jeff Oxman, 2009.
An Amazing Dollar Die, by Leroy Van Allen, *Numismatist,* June 2003.

1878 P VAM 7 Gouge A

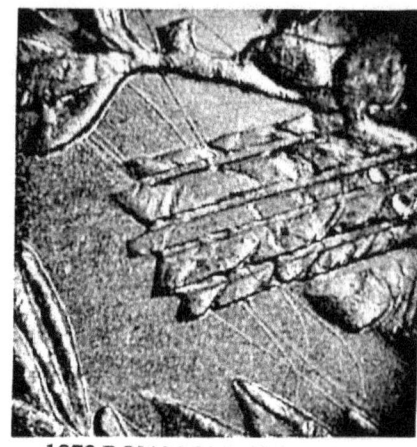

1878 P VAM 80 Polishing Lines
Arrow Feathers

1878 CC VAM 11 Scratches in Wing

1878 S VAM 1D Scratches in
Tail Feathers

1878 S VAM 19 Die Gouge Cap

1879 S VAM 29 Die Gouge Hair

1880 O VAM 48 Hangnail Eagle

1881 O VAM 1D Flaky Eye

1881 O VAM 43 Die Gouge DOL

1882 CC VAM 2D Die Gouges OLL

1888 P VAM 7 Die Gouges Above Wing

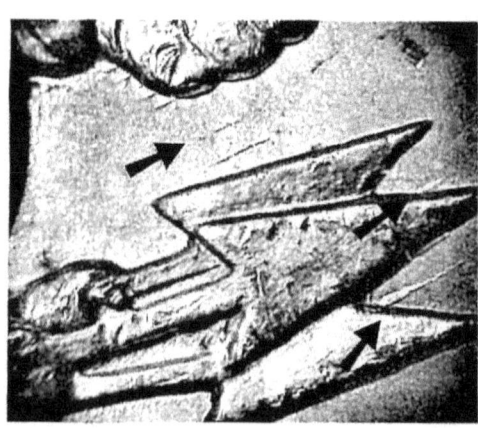

1888 P VAM 7A Gouges Arrow Heads

1888 P VAM 7 Die Gouges Tail Feathers

1888 O VAM 7A Die Gouges Star

1888 S VAM 13 Die Gouges Wing

1888 S VAM 13 Gouges on Tail Feathers

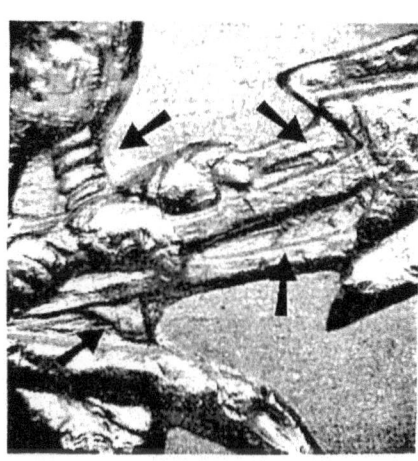

1888 S VAM 13 Gouges Arrow Shafts

1890 CC VAM 4 Tail Bar

1888 S VAM 13 Gouges Below Talons

1889 P VAM 52 Die Gouge Neck

1901 P VAM 2A Die Gouge E

1890 O VAM 10 Comet Die Gouges

1891 S VAM 9A Die Gouges Lower Reverse

1900 O VAM 2A Scratches Wheat Leaves

1902 O VAM 5A Vertical Die Scratches

1902 O VAM 50 Vertical Die Scratches

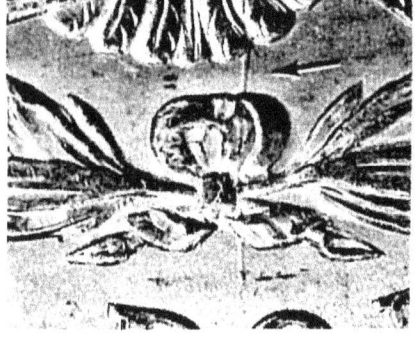

1921 P VAM 1C Die Gouge
Wreath Bow

1921 P VAM 3A Die Gouge Tail Feathers

1921 P VAM 3F Die Gouge Wing

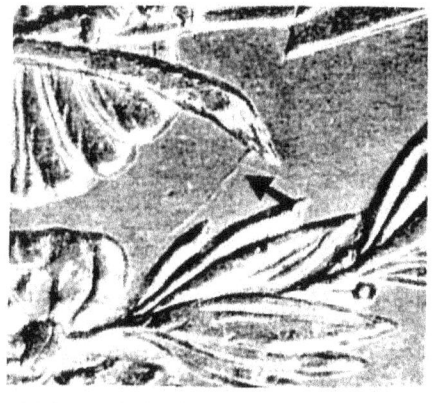

1921 P VAM 16 Die Gouge Olive Branch

1921 P VAM 3U Pierced Neck Gouge

1921 D VAM 1S Die Gouges TED

1921 S VAM 6A Die Gouge BU

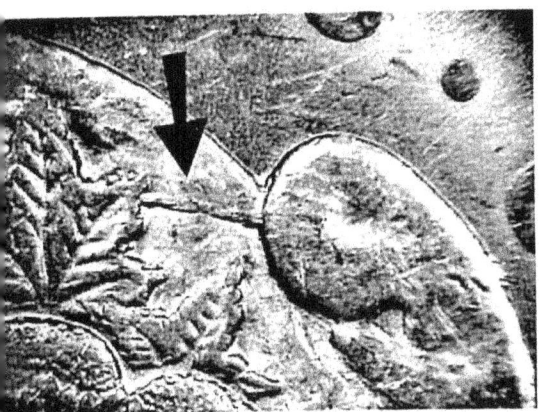

1921 S VAM 1B1 Die Gouge Cap
First Die State

1921 S VAM 1B1 Die Gouge Cap Back
First Die State

19212 S VAM 1B4 Die Gouge IB
Fifth Die State

21 S VAM 1B3 Thorn Head Die Gouges
Third Die State

1921 S VAM 1B5 Die Gouges IB
Eighth Die State

1921 S VAM 1B7 Die Gouges LIBERTY & Cap
Tenth Die State

Denticle Impressions

Denticle impressions are **raised dots**, usually in the **shape of a triangle**, that occur in the coin **fields**, typically in a **line**. They have the **same spacing** between the dots as the **denticles** near the coin edge. These raised dots were caused by the **accidental impact** of another die **raised triangle shaped denticle spaces**.

The raised dots denticle impressions were first reported in 2001 and since then over 40 different dies have been reported with them. All except one obverse die have the denticle impressions on the reverse dies. Most have two rows of four the seven raised dots in a line with the outer and inner denticle space edges producing the two rows. Most also appear below the eagle's tail feathers but there are cases of them at the left, right and top sides of the reverse die. There is even an 1878 S with denticle impressions on the obverse at the edge of the Liberty head neck and at the date. Most are fairly shallow and faint.

It is thought that the denticle impressions were caused as the upper obverse die was being installed in a coining press. Because the dies were hardened, only another hardened die would have made the denticle impressions. Morgan dollar working dies were well protected when in storage or in transit in compartmented wooden boxes. The Morgan reverse die was the lower one in a coining press within the collar and the obverse die was the upper hammer one.

If during the **installation** or **removal** of the **upper obverse die** from the coining press, the workman **accidently contacted the exposed lower reverse die face**, the denticle space edges could have been **transferred** as **two lines of raised dots** in the reverse exposed and raised **die fields**. The vertical space between the obverse and reverse dies in the coining press was very short and any brush, tick or drop of a tilted upper obverse die could have caused the denticle impressions on the lower reverse die fields.

The accompanying photographs show samples of some known denticle impressions. The number of denticle impressions dies are about the same for the Philadelphia and New Orleans Mints and considerable less for the San Francisco Mint. Perhaps the latter had more careful die installers or the coining presses were of a different design with better access to the dies. There are a few examples of only one or two denticle impressions, but most have 4-7 raised dots in a line and some below in another line. The 1890 P has the most listed denticle impressions die varieties, currently at eight.

The most denticle impressions on a coin, by far, is an **1878 S VAM 17** with a total of **56.** It is also the first reported denticle impressions die in 2001. There are **43** on the **reverse** with 18 around OLL in DOLLAR, four below the tail feathers and the rest around UNITED STATES. The **obverse** has **five** impressions at the Liberty head neck and **eight** at the date and is the only known obverse so far with denticle impressions.

Available references–
Denticle Impressions Morgan Dollar Attribution Guide, by Leroy Van Allen, September 2009.
Official Guide to the Morgan Dollar Hit List 40, by Jeff Oxman, 2009.

878 S VAM 17B Denticle Impressions

878 S VAM 17B Denticle Impressions Date

1878 P VAM 225A Denticle Impressions

1890 O VAM 1C Denticle Impressions

1921 P VAM 31A1 Denticle Impressions

1878 S VAM 17B Denticle Impressions OLL

1878 S VAM 17B Denticle Impressions Neck

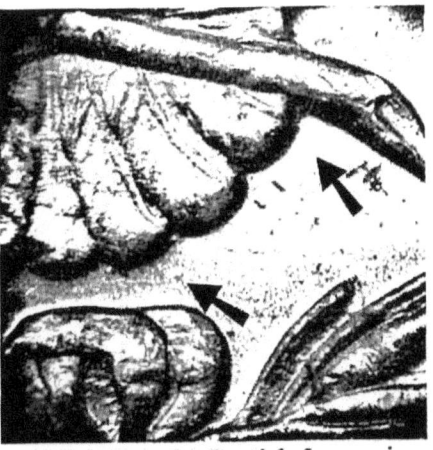

1888 P VAM 17A Denticle Impressions

1901 O VAM 11 Denticle Impressions

1878 S VAM 17C Denticle Impressions AT

1887 P VAM 1E Denticle Impressions

1890 P VAM 4A Denticle Impressions

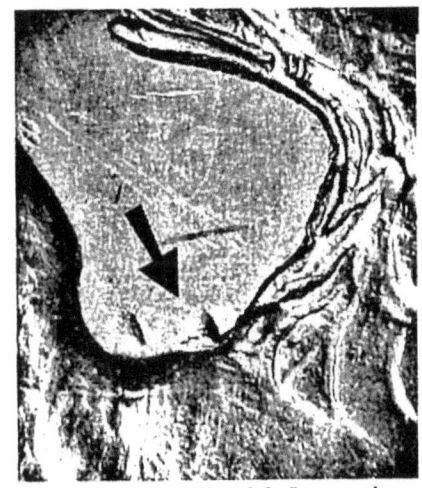

1901 O VAM 45 2 Denticle Impressions

Thread-Like Die Impressions

These thread-like die impressions are **raised** and usually **curved fine lines** on the **coin devices**. They don't occur in the die fields because they would have been polished away by the basining and polishing of the die face before they were placed into service in the coining presses. The thread-like die impressions can be differentiated from die scratches because the latter are usually straight or varying widths and the **thread-like die impressions** are **curvy** with about the **same width as fine threads**.

As expected, the thread-like die impressions were actually made on the working dies during the hubbing of the design into the die. It took 7 to 10 hubbing blows to transfer the entire design across the Morgan working die face. In-between each hubbing blow, the dies had to be annealed to soften the work hardened metal. Both the hub face and die face had to be cleaned before the hubbing blow. **Cloth rags** would have been **used to wipe the hub and die faces**. Any **fine threads left** on the **hub** or **die face** by the cloth would subsequently be **impressed into the softened die face**, but not into the hardened hub face.

The thread-like die impressions can take many shapes with some having just a gentle curve, while others may have one or several loops. Being cloth threads, they are not very thick in diameter. They can also be long or short but will always have a curve or some sort. Many of the thread-like die impressions are small and short and not very visible to the naked eye, but may be listed as die markers. Others can be fairly long and bold that may be listed as sub-varieties, such as the **1879 S VAM 36 'Cootie'** shaped die impression. Although interesting, most thread-like die impressions serve as a minor part of the die variety listings or as die markers.

Thread-like die impressions are fairly scarce and not nearly as prevalent as die scratches and gouges. However, they seldom bring premium prices just for this interesting die variety, as they aren't very visible to the naked eye. The accompanying photographs show some examples of various dates that have thread-like die impressions.

1878 P VAM 141A Thread-Like Impression

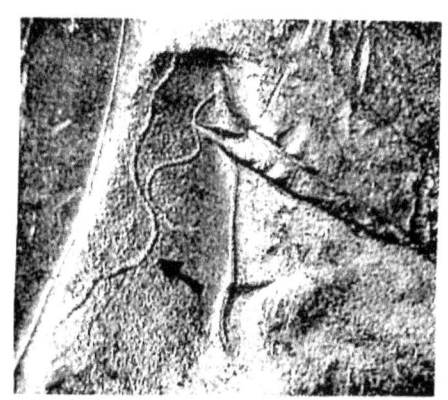

1879 P VAM 41 Worm Eye Die Impressions

1879 S VAM 26 Thread-Like Impressions Behind Eye

1879 S VAM 36 Cootie Die Impression

1884 P VAM 8D Hair Impression Jaw

1884 P VAM 14 Extra Forehead Curl

1887 O VAM 38 Thread-Like
Vee Impression

1888 P VAM 8 Thread-Like Impression

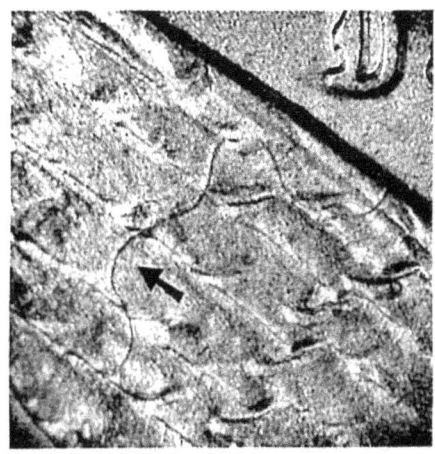

1889 P VAM 29 Thread-Like Impression

1896 P VAM 1C Thread-Like Impression

1896 S VAM 1A Thread-Like Impression

1898 P VAM 2C Thread-Like Impression
Cotton Leaf

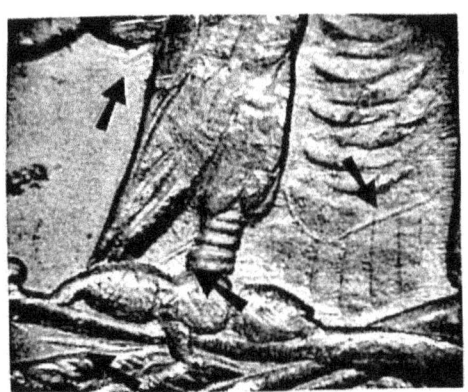

1901 O VAM 6B Die Gouges,
Thread-Like Impression

1902 O VAM 12 Thread-Like Impression Wing

Overlapping Reeding

As explained in the section on **Edge Reeding**, a flat steel plate **collar** with grooves on the inside of the hole produced the edge reeding on the coin. When the planchet was struck by the obverse and reverse dies, the metal expanded sideways into the collar grooves producing the edge reeding. A tapered cylinder with groves and ridges along it's sides called a **swaging** or **reeding tool** was forced into the collar blank to produce the groves on the inside of the collar hole. A milling machine made the grooves on the cylinder. The number of grooves around the cylinder was determined by setting the index spacing of the milling machine.

If the index spacing was not properly set, then the milling machine would not produce **exactly superimposed groves** at the **start and finish** grooves on the cylinder. This would cause the grooves at the start-finish point to **not exactly merge**. They would **overlap** and **fade on either side** of the **start-finish point** where the milling tool entered against the cylinder and then left the surface. An example of this overlapping reeding is shown for the **1892 O**. Note that the grooves fade away in either direction and the middle section shows very narrow ridges and grooves where they were not exactly superimposed.

Overlapping reeding is only known to occur on **six** years of the **New Orleans** minted coins: **1883, 1884, 1892, 1900, 1901 and 1904.** Apparently the New Orleans Mint machinist operating the milling machine wasn't always skilled at merging the start and finish grooves. Most of the overlapping reeding occurs at two locations. A few only have the overlapping reeding at one location and some have three locations. The machinist started and stopped at several locations around the swaging tool cylinder that caused multiple overlapping reeding.

Two of the five 1883 O overlapping reeding varieties show **shifting** of the **overlapping reeding locations** on different coins of the same die variety. Four of the seven 1884 O overlapping reeding varieties show shifting of their locations, but some of these may be due to multiple dies for one listing. Both of the two 1892 O overlapping reeding varieties show shifting locations. The single 1900 O and 1904 O overlapping reeding varieties show shifting locations but the one 1901 O overlapping reeding variety shows only one fixed location. The **shifting of overlapping reeding locations** on a die variety was **due to a loose collar** in the coining press that rotated during the striking of coins of a particular die pair.

The accompanying photographs show some examples of overlapping reeding for various dates.

Available references–
1904 O Morgan Dollar Series Attribution Guide, by Alan Scott, 2010.

3 O VAM 51 Overlapping Reeding 2 O'clock

1883 O VAM 58 Overlapping Reeding 3 O'clock

1884 O VAM 42B Overlapping Reeding
4 O'clock

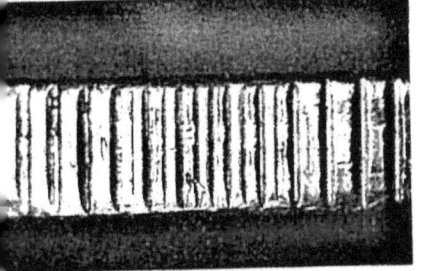

83 O VAM 51 Overlapping Reeding 5 O'clock

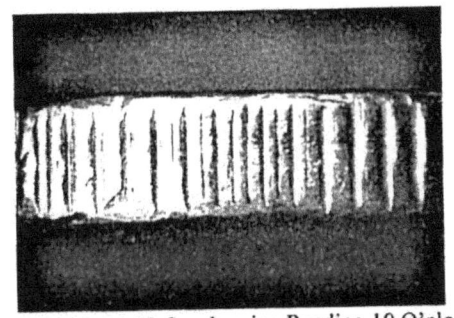

1883 O VAM 58 Overlapping Reeding 10 O'clock

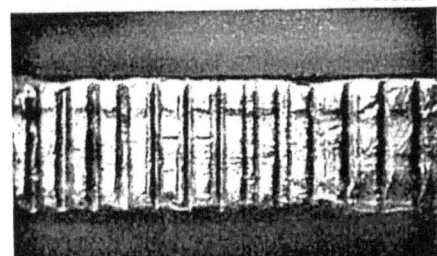

1884 O VAM 42B Overlapping Reeding
11 O'clock

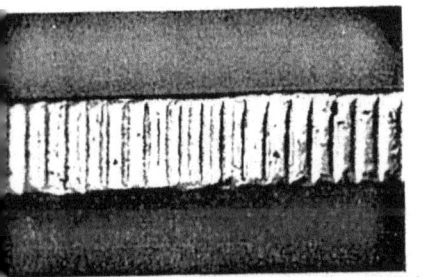

92 O VAM 12 Overlapping Reeding 3 O'clock

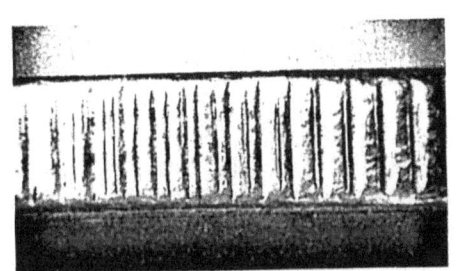

1900 O VAM 50 Overlapping Reeding 8 O'clock

1901 O VAM 54 Overlapping Reeding 4 O'clock

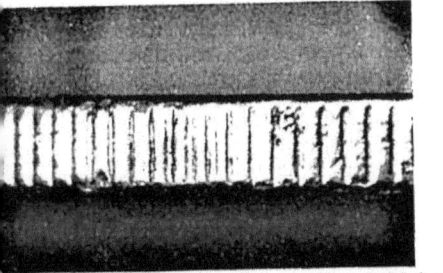

892 O VAM 12 Overlapping Reeding 9 O'clock

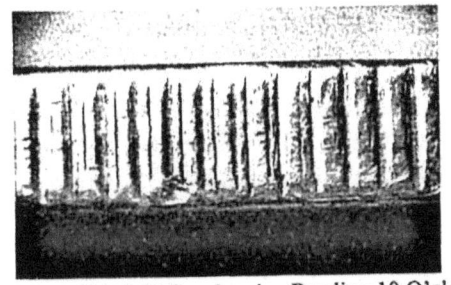

1900 O VAM 50 Overlapping Reeding 10 O'clock

1901 O VAM 54 Overlapping Reeding
5:30 O'clock

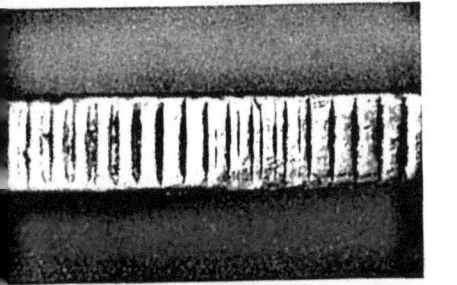

892 O VAM 12 Overlapping Reeding 11 O'clock

1900 O VAM 50 Overlapping Reeding 11 O'clock

1904 O VAM 22A2 Overlapping Reeding
12 O'clock

1904 O VAM 22A2 Overlapping Reeding
7:30 O'clock

INTENTIONAL DIE FLAWS

These changes in the normal die design are considered die varieties since they were intentionally performed on the working dies to extend their usage, repair flaws, identify specific dies and improve the designs. It is another large category of die changes and includes many die varieties. The punching of a later date over an earlier date working die to further their use resulted in **many over dates** in **1880** and **two overdates in 1887**. There are also two years where the reverse mint mark was changed so another mint could use the dies for the years **1882 O/S** and **1900 O/CC**. Many dies were repaired using **touch up engraving** on the eagle's wing and tail feathers for the **1878 P & S** and **1879 S** dies. And the San Francisco Mint even used **acid** on several dies of **1878, 1879** and **1882** in an attempt to repair over polished areas. Even more **amazing** is the recent discovery that most of the **1921 P, D & S** working dies had **scribbling die scratches** applied at the eagle's right leg in a half-hearted attempt to repair the over polished tail feather there. It is known that over 50 Morgan obverse working dies had **partial date digits** punched into the **denticles** below the date and elsewhere as a test to determine if the working dies had been softened prior to punching in the complete date. Some working dies had special **raised dots** punched into them for presumably identifying purposes on a few **1884 P** and **1921 P, D & S** working dies. Many dies from **1884 thru 1886** had a **dash index mark** punched above the tenth denticle from the Liberty head neck point as a guide of where to punch the right 8 into the die. There are also many examples of **dual hub dies** in 1878 and later from **1900 thru 1904** where earlier design working dies were re-hubbed with a later design hub to improve their usage.

Date Digit Design and Sizes

The date digit punches were all made by hand for the Morgan dollar. This resulted in slight variations in their design over the years as the punches worn out and were replaced. The **most significant change** in the date digits occurred in **1884** and the later years when the **date size** was **reduced** and the **width of all digits** was made **slightly less**.

Although each numeral had at least two and up to four variations, they are of **minor** significance. A particular digit design was apparently used for an entire year even when used for a number of years. There are no obvious intermixing of digit designs for a particular year. Therefore, die variety listings have **not occurred** specifically for date digit design variations.

1882 CC VAM 2C Large Wide Digits

1886 Proof VAM 15 Small Narrow Digits

Overdates

There are two different years with known overdates for the Morgan dollars. These are **1880** with **80/79** type overdates and **1887** with **7/6** type overdates. **Twenty-three** different **1880** overdate dies have been identified for the Philadelphia, Carson City, New Orleans and San Francisco Mint struck coins. There is **one each** 7/6 overdate for the **1887** Philadelphia and New Orleans struck coins.

Overdates were the result of salvaging the obverse working dies left over from a previous year by punching in the following year's digit(s) so the expensive working dies could be utilized. The overdate dies were modified at the Philadelphia Mint since it prepared the Morgan dollar working dies for all of the mints. The 1880 overdates were discovered during 1964-1967 and again in 1976-1977 when some additional overdates on the surface of 80 digits were discovered. The 1887 overdates were discovered in 1972 and early 1973.

Remnants of the **1880** overdates with underlying 79 digits show all or portions of the **7** as the **seven crossbar** and **stem** inside the 8 loops, **spikes** above the top of the 8 from the 7 upper serifs, a **dash** below the 8 and a **checkmark** on the left side of the 8 upper loop from the left side of the seven crossbar. Remnants of the **9** show as **loops** and raised metal inside the 0 on a couple dies and on the **surface** on one die. For the **1887** overdate, the 6 remnants show primarily as **curved lines** on both sides of the 7 bottom.

The **1880 P** has **four strong** overdates showing the 7 spikes above the 8, crossbar within the 8 upper loop and remnants of the 7 and 9 on top of the 80 digits. There are three dies that only show the 7 checkmark on the 8 upper loop surface and two weak ones with small raised metal within the 8 loops.

By far, the **strongest overdates** of the entire Morgan dollar series are **three** of the **1880 CC** overdates. **VAM 4** shows both the **7 and 9 clearly** within the 80 and checkmark of the 8 upper loop. **VAMs 5** and **6** show a **clear 7** within the 8 and checkmark on the 8 upper loop but nothing inside the 0. A fourth 1880 CC die shows a faint 7 spike at top left outside plus some vertical raised bar inside the loop and dash below the 8. Although the 1880 CC has the three strongest overdates, the General Services Administration (GSA) sold 115,000 uncirculated 1880 CC in the 1970's with the strong overdates plentiful in that hoard.

The **1880 O** has **two strong** overdate dies with crossbars in the 8 upper loop, faint ear above the 8 and checkmark on the surface of the 8 upper loop. There is one die with a strong spike at top outside and checkmark on the 8 upper loop. Three dies show only the 7 checkmark on the 8 upper loop.

One of the **1880 S** dies shows raised metal in most of the 8 upper loop and some raised metal at the upper right inside of the 0. Another die shows two horizontal lines in the 8 upper loop of the 7 crossbar. A third die shows a 7 checkmark of the 8 upper loop and a faint spike at the top left of the 8. A fourth die is somewhat controversial as an overdate with wide raised metal within the 0 that has polishing lines that resembles the remnants of the 9 within the 0 of the 1880 CC VAM 4 overdate.

The **1887 P** overdate shows a **strong curved line** of the bottom of the 6 to the right of the 7 bottom of the vertical stem, a short bar on the lower left side and a short vertical spike at the very top of the 7 crossbar. The **1887 O** overdate shows a **long curved line** at the bottom right of the 7 and a short line on the lower left side.

Available references–
Overdates & Over Mint Marks of Morgan Dollars Attribution Guide, by Leroy Van Allen, Revised March 2009.
Carson City Morgan Dollars, by Adam Crum, Selby Ungar and Jeff Oxman, Whitman Publishing, 2010.
Morgan Silver Dollars, by Q. David Bowers, Whitman Publishing, 2004.
Top 100 Morgan Dollar Varieties: The VAM Keys, by Michael Fey & Jeff Oxman, 4th ed., 2009.
SSDC Official Guide to the Hot 50 Morgan Dollar Varieties, by Jeff Oxman, 2000.
Official Guide to the Morgan Dollar Hit List 40, by Jeff Oxman, 2009.

1880 P VAM 6 8/7 Spikes

1880 P VAM 7 8/7 Crossbar

1880 P VAM 8 8/7 Ears

1880 P VAM 23 80/79

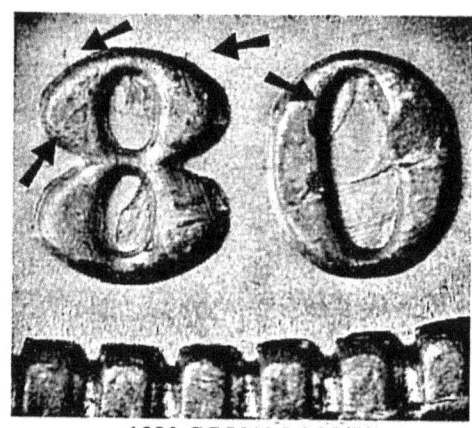

1880 CC VAM 4 80/79

1880 CC VAM 5 8/7 High

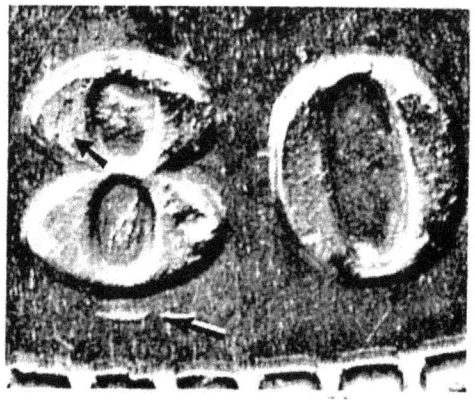

1880 CC VAM 6 8/7 Low

1880 O VAM 4 80/79

1880 O VAM 5 8/7 Ear

1880 O VAM 6C 8/7 Spike

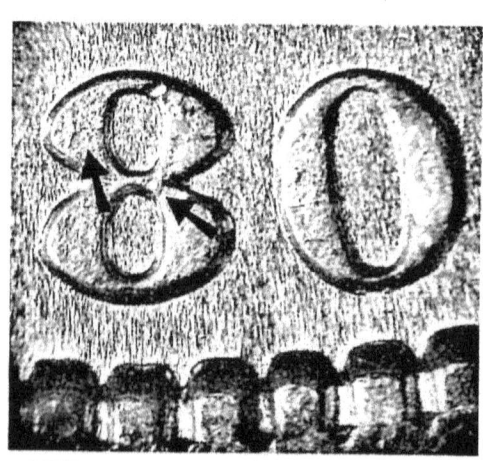

1880 O VAM 16/17/63 8/7 Checkmark

1880 S VAM 8 80/79 Ear

1880 S VAM 10 8/7 Crossbar

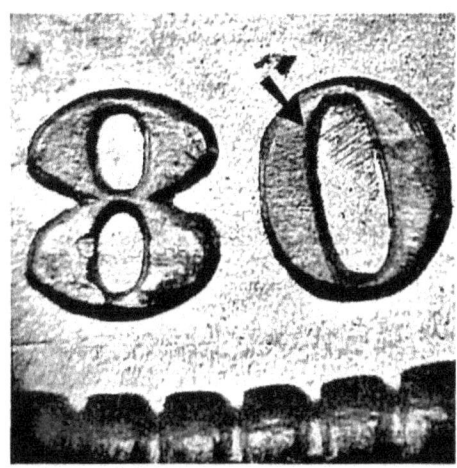

1880 S VAM 11 0/9

1887 P VAM 2 7/6

1880 S VAM 12 8/7 Spike, Checkmark

1887 O VAM 3 7/6

Dash Below Date

A **strange mark below the date digits** is found on quite a few working dies from **1879 thru 1886.** They are a **short horizontal dash below the right 8** and always above the **tenth denticle** from the Liberty head neck point. They do vary somewhat in distance below the bottom of the 8. Some dashes are very thick and adjacent to the bottom of the right 8. Many are faint from the basining and polishing of the dies.

The mint worker who punched the date digits into the working dies counted over ten denticles from the Liberty head neck point and used a small rectangular punch to place the dash mark above that denticle. Apparently this index mark dash was used as a **guide** to **punch the right 8 lateral position** so the **spacing would be consistent** between the digits when the two right digits were punched into the working die from 1879 thru 1883. From 1884 thru 1886 the dash index was used to **position the entire date lateral position.** However, because of the smaller date digits and narrower date from 1884 onwards, this resulted in the left edge of the 1 base being further from the neck point than the previous years of over the third denticle. After 1886, the dash index below the right 8 was no longer used and the **date lateral position varied** over a wide range from very near to very far.

The accompanying photographs show a representative sample of the dash below the dates. One of the largest dashes is the **1885 CC VAM 4.** Another thick dash is the **1885 P VAM 8/22.** Most dashes under the right 8 don't add a premium price, except for the very thick and visible dashes.

Available references–
SSDC Official Guide to the Hot 50 Morgan Dollar Varieties, by Jeff Oxman, 2000.
Official Guide to the Morgan Dollar Hit List 40, by Jeff Oxman, 2009.

1879 P VAM 26 Doubled Date, Dash

1880 O VAM 11 Dash Under Date

1880 O VAM 3 Dash Under 8

1880 S VAM 13 Dash Under 8

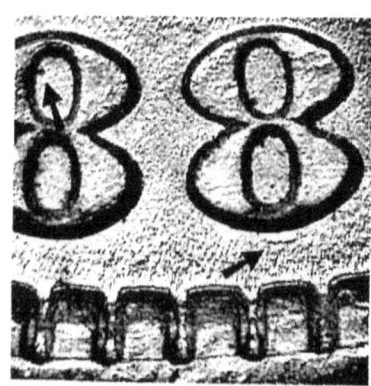

1881 O VAM 17 Dash Under 8

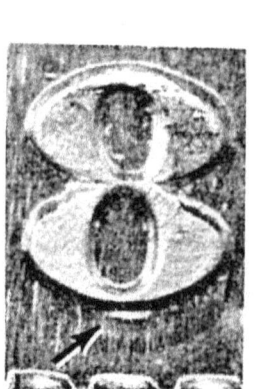

1881 S VAM 3 Dash Under 8

1882 O VAM 30 Dash Under 8

1883 P VAM 2 Dash Under 8

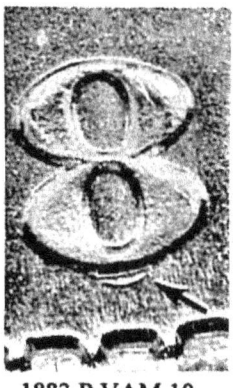

1883 P VAM 10
Dash Under 8

1883 CC VAM 3 Dash Under 8

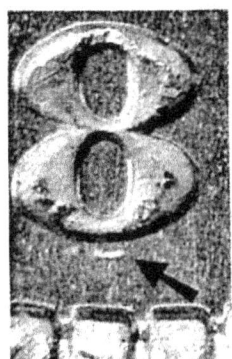

1883 O VAM 2
Dash Under 8

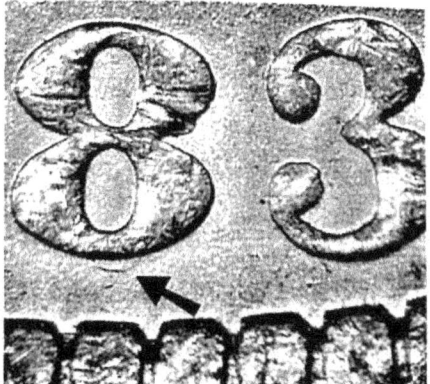

1883 O VAM 32 Dash Under 8

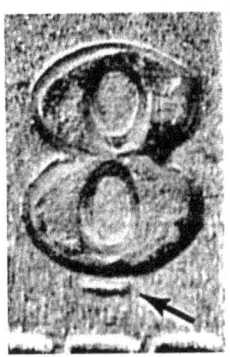

1884 P VAM 2
Dash Under 8

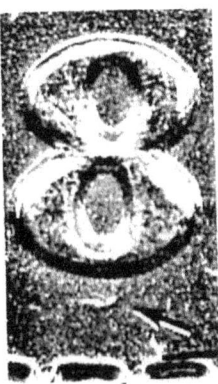

1884 P VAM 6
Dash Under 8

1884 P VAM 7 Slanted Dash Under 8

1885 P VAM 4 Low Dash Under 8

1885 P VAM 18 High Dash Under 8

1885 P VAM 22 Thick Dash
Under 8

1885 P VAM 29
High Dash Set Left

1885 CC VAM 4 Thick Dash Under 8

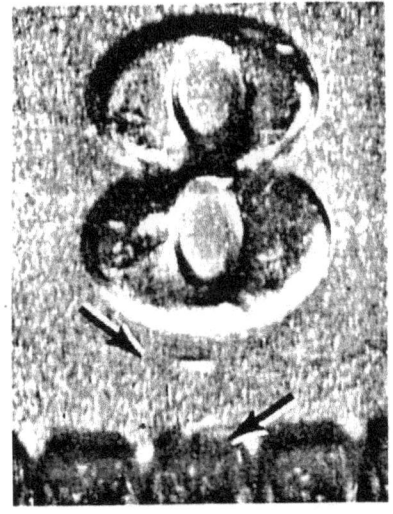

1885 O VAM 7 Dash Under 8,
Line in Denticles

1886 Proof VAM 15 Dash Under 8

Misplaced Date Digits

Misplaced date digits are **portions of the digits** that appear on dies **away from the usual area of the date**. For the Morgan dollar, the date was below the truncated Liberty head neck and lower hair and above the denticles at the rim. There was **quite a bit of latitude** in the **lateral position** with the left side of the 1 two to four denticles from the neck point and **close to the denticles** up to **close to the neck truncation**.

The abbreviated term for **misplaced date of MPD** is currently widely used. However, it is very rare that all four date digits are found misplaced, with single or two digits most common for Morgan dollar MPDs. Perhaps MPD should be referred as **misplaced digits**.

Most of the Morgan dollar MPDs are found with **only the tops of digits** showing as **curved or straight raised bars in the denticle spaces below the date.** A few isolated cases show the bottom or top of digits in the space between the date and denticles. And there are a couple examples of the bottom of a digit showing in the hair edge above the date.

There are currently over 70 known examples of MPDs for the Morgan dollars. They have occurred on about 40 different date/mint mark combinations from 1879 thru 1903 with continuous date examples from 1879 thru 1892. The first Morgan dollar recognized with a MPD was reported in 1990 with most MPDs being reported from 1998 and later. They are highly collectable die varieties with some being listed as **Top 100** and **Hit List 40** varieties. There are even two **proof** Morgan dollars of 1888 and 1900 with MPDs in the denticles.

Generally, single digit tops in the denticles are only listed if there are **raised curved bars** in **two adjacent spaces**, unless the raised curved bar is **unusually bold and clear in one denticle space**. Most MPD listings are for the top of a single digit in the denticles. But there a number with two digits, quite a few with three digits but only one example with four digit tops showing. The Morgan dollar dates were punched into the working dies by hand using singe digit punches and multiple digit logotypes.

A **possible reason for MPDs** on Morgan dollar working dies was that the tops of the date digits were lightly punched into a convenient inconspicuous location of denticles or hair edge near the date location **to determine if the dies had been annealed**. Hubbing of the working dies work hardened them and they had to be annealed to soften the die metal before the date were punched in. Punching the date into hardened dies would have damaged the valuable digit punches. A separate die annealing facility on a different floor from the engraving room at the Philadelphia Mint in use up until 1901 likely required testing a single die in a box of 20 to 40 dies to determine if they were annealed.

Some example MPDs are shown in the accompanying photographs. The **first reported** Morgan dollar MPD in **1990** was the **1896 P VAM 19** with 8 top in the denticles. A nice three digit MPD of 900 in the denticles is the **1900 P VAM 16.** Even a **1900 Proof VAM 32** has a clear 0 in the denticles. The **1888 O VAM 28** shows the top of a 1 in two denticle spaces. The tops of 18 in the denticles is shown for the **1884 S VAM 8.** A bottom of a 9 shows at the **edge of the lower hair** for the **1892 O VAM 12.** Similarly, the **1886 P VAM 21** shows the bottom of an 8 **below the designer's initial M.** One of the clearest MPDs is the **1882 CC VAM 2** with the **1 top in the field** between the bottom of 8 and denticles. An **unusual** MPD is the **1882 P VAM 24** with a **double 1 base below** the left 8.

Available references–

Misplaced Date Digits Morgan Dollar Attribution Guide, by Leroy Van Allen and Bill Van Note, revised January 2009.

Morgan Dollar Overdate, Over Mintmarks, Misplaced Dates, and Clashed E Reverses, by Kevin Flynn, Archive Press, 1998.

Carson City Morgan Dollars, by Adam, Selby Ungar & Jeff Oxman, Whitman Publishing, 2010.

Top 100 Morgan Dollar Varieties: The VAM Keys, by Michael Fey & Jeff Oxman, 4th ed., 2009.

Official Guide to the Morgan Dollar Hit List 40, by Jeff Oxman, 2009.

1881 S VAM 52 8 in Denticles

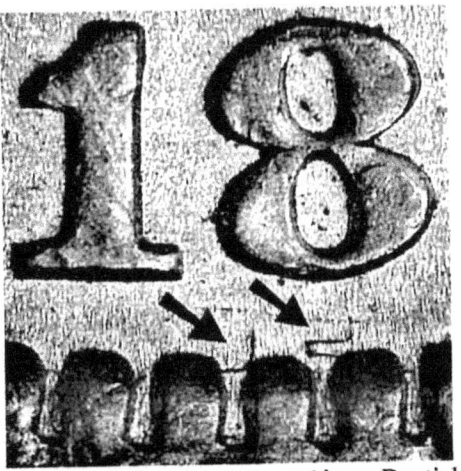

1882 P VAM 24 Double 1 Base Above Denticles

1882 CC VAM 2 1 Top Below 8

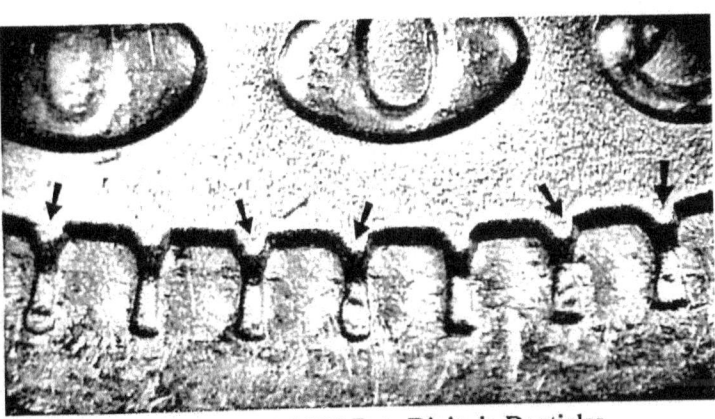

1883 O VAM 39 Date Digits in Denticles

1884 O VAM 25 188 in Denticles

1884 S VAM 9 884 in Denticles

1884 S VAM 8 18 in Denticles

1885 P VAM 6 85 in Denticles

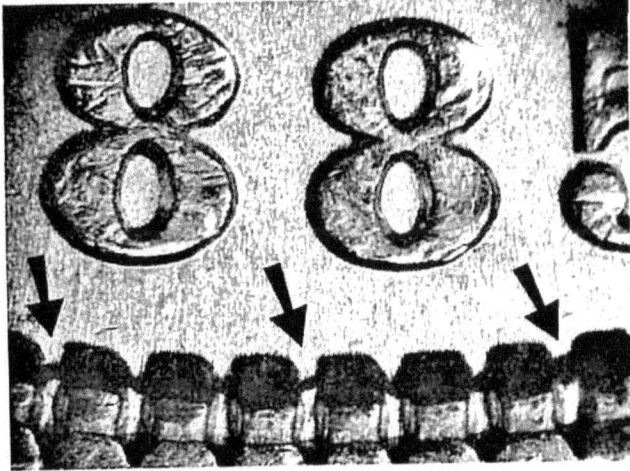

1885 P VAM 32 885 in Denticles

1885 O VAM 28 1 in Denticles

1886 P VAM 21 8 Base Below M

1888 O VAM 9 18 in Denticles

1888 O VAM 28 1 in Denticles

1888 O VAM 35 18 in Denticles

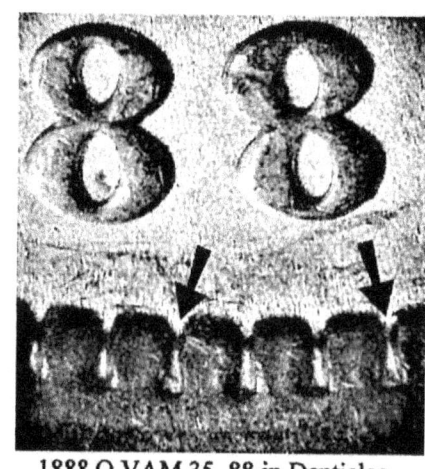

1888 O VAM 35 88 in Denticles

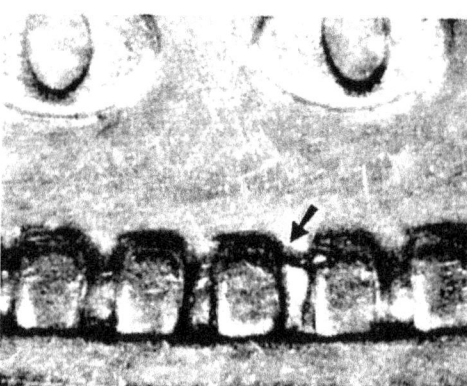

1888 Proof VAM 25 8 in Denticles

1892 O VAM 12 9 Below Hair

1896 P VAM 19 8 in Denticles

1900 Proof VAM 32 0 in Denticles

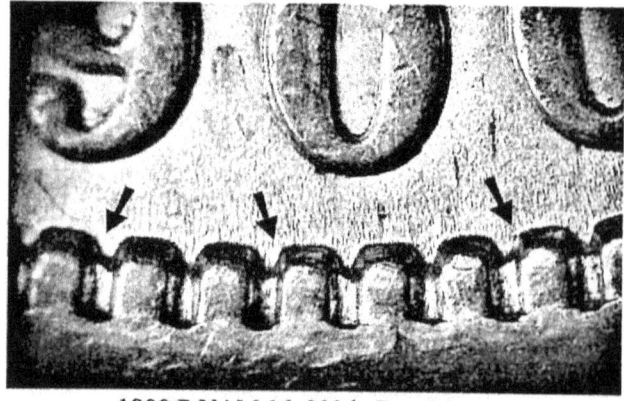

1900 P VAM 16 900 in Denticles

1903 S VAM 6 903 in Denticles

Mint Mark Sizes

There were **four branch mints** that struck the Morgan dollar: Carson City, Denver, New Orleans and San Francisco. Their mint marks were punched into the working dies by hand at the Philadelphia Mint **below the reverse wreath bow**. The **San Francisco Mint** struck coins thru-out the Morgan dollar series from 1878 thru 1904 and in 1921. **Six different S mint marks** were used, the most of any branch mint. They ranged greatly in size from the small micro S only used in 1921 up to a very large one only used in 1880 and on some Seated Liberty dollars. Most years used a medium size S with pointed serfs from 1879 thru 1900. A small square S was used in 1878 and for some 1879 dies. A large wide S with more rounded top and bottom serifs was used from 1899 thru 1904. An **anomaly** occurred for one **1903 die** that had a **small round S** that was **used on Barber quarters** and it is quite scarce.

The **New Orleans Mint** struck coins from 1879 thru 1904. **Four different size O mint marks** were used ranging in size from a small micro O used in 1880 and 1899 on Seated Liberty and Barber quarters to a large oval O only used in 1879. A tall oval medium O with narrow slit was used from 1879 thru 1884 and on a few dies again in 1888 and 1889. However, the narrow slit tended to fill up on the dies when the mint mark was punched in. So a medium O mint mark with wide opening was used from 1884 thru 1904. It should be mentioned that the **small micro O mint mark** also appears on some scarce **circulated counterfeit** 1896 O, 1900 O, 1901 O & 1902 O.

The **Carson City Mint** struck coins from 1878 thru 1885 and again from 1889 thru 1893. There were only **two basic size C mint marks** used for the Carson City Mint. A small size C was used in 1878 and on some 1880 dies that was same one used for the Seated Liberty dollars. Two C's were punched into the die individually that resulted in different spacing between them. A large C was used from 1879 thru 1885 and again in 1889 thru 1893. These two large C's were generally punched into the die simultaneously as their spacing and individual orientation didn't vary much, except for a few cases.

The **Denver Mint** only struck coins in 1921. Only **one size D mint mark** was used for the Denver Mint dies that was a small micro size.

The accompanying photographs the various mint marks sizes.

Available references–
Top 100 Morgan Dollar Varieties: The VAM Keys, by Michael Fey & Jeff Oxman, 4th ed., 2009.
The Oval O Coins of 1888 and 1889, An Attribution Guide, by C. Ash Harrison, 2006.

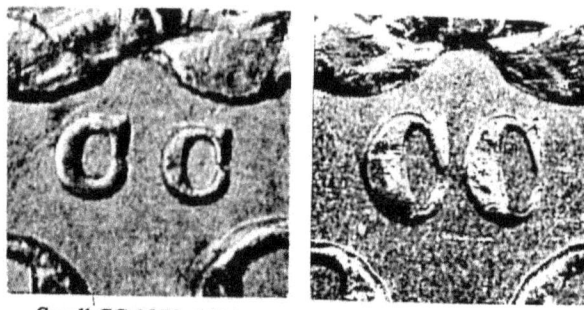

Small CC 1878, 1880   Large CC 1879-1885, 1889-1893

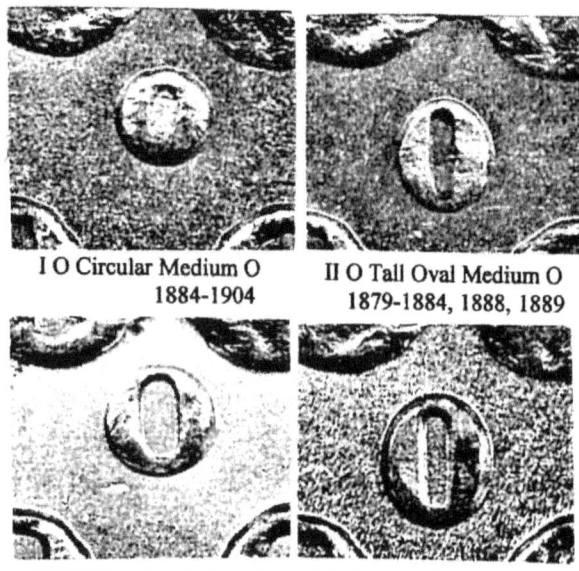

I O Circular Medium O
1884-1904

II O Tall Oval Medium O
1879-1884, 1888, 1889

III O Circular Medium O
1884-1904

IV O Large Oval O 1879

I D Micro D 1921

I S Micro S 1921   II S Small Round S 1903   III S Small Square S 1878, 1879

IV S Medium S 1879-1900   V S Large S 1899-1904   VI S Very Large S 1880

Over Mint Marks

There are **four different dates** with **two different mint marks showing, 1879 CC, 1882 O, 1900 O and 1900 S**. The **1882 O** and **1900 O** have a **different underlying mint mark of S** for the **1882 O** and **CC for the 1900 O**. The 1900 O/CC over mint mark was first reported in The Numismatist in November 1928 by Will W. Neil and the 1882 O/S over mint mark by Francis Klaes in his pamphlet, *Die Varieties of Morgan Silver Dollars,* June 1963. **Different size mint mark** are **under the normal size mint mark** for the **1879 CC** and **1900 S**.

Three different O/S over mint marks exist for the **1882 O** with **diagonal bars showing within** the **O mint mark** and one also shows a partial S serif at the lower left outside. There are **five different 1900 O with O/CC over mint marks** that comprise six different die variety listings. One die shows almost the complete remains including the serifs of both C's to the left and right outside of the O mint mark. A couple other dies show most of the C curves without the serifs.

The modification of five reverse dies with CC mint mark to a bolder O mint mark for six die combinations would have been performed at the Philadelphia Mint. The Carson City Mint suspended coining operations on June 1, 1893 because of the repeal of the Sherman Act in 1893 that had authorized coinage of large amounts of silver dollars. The greatly reduced silver dollar coinage resulted in the Carson City Mint only having it's refinery department remain open. The higher coining costs of the Carson City Mint compared to the San Francisco Mint and because the San Francisco Mint could handle all of the western mines silver output resulted in the closing of the Carson City Mint facility in 1899. The mint machinery was dismantled and shipped to the Philadelphia Mint in 1899. Left over CC dies were then modified with the O mint mark for use by the New Orleans Mint which had the highest silver dollar production of all the mints in 1900.

The **1979 CC** has a **large pair of CC mint marks over a smaller pair of CC mint marks** and is called the **"Capped CC"**. However, the underlying smaller CC mint marks are not very clear except for the top of the loops because of roughness inside the large CC's. This was apparently an attempt to remove part of the small CC loops.

There is a **narrow S mint mark over a wide S mint mark** for the **1900 S** with portions of the wide S loops showing to the upper left and lower right outside of the narrow S. Both size S mint marks were used during 1899 and 1900. Early die states don't show the underlying side S, so the wide S loops must have later chipped out of the die from die stress of striking coins.

Available references–
Overdates and Over Mint Mrks of Morgan Dollars Attribution Guide, by Leroy Van Allen, Revised
    March 2009.
1900 O Over CC Attribution Guide, by C. Ash Harrison, 2006.
Top 100 Morgan Dollar Varieties: The VAM Keys, by Michael Fey & Jeff Oxman, 4th ed., 2009.

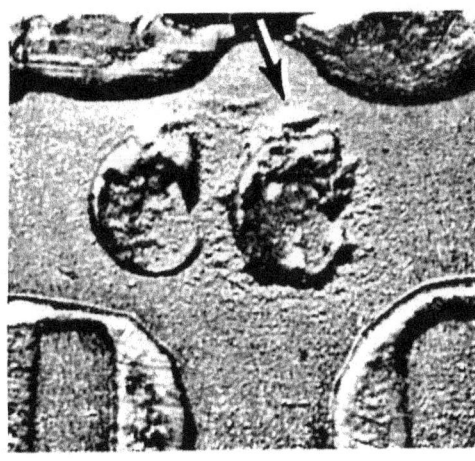

1879 CC VAM 3 Large Over Small CC

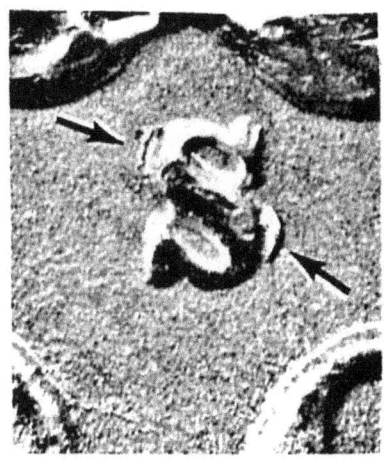

1900 S VAM 3 Wide Over Narrow S

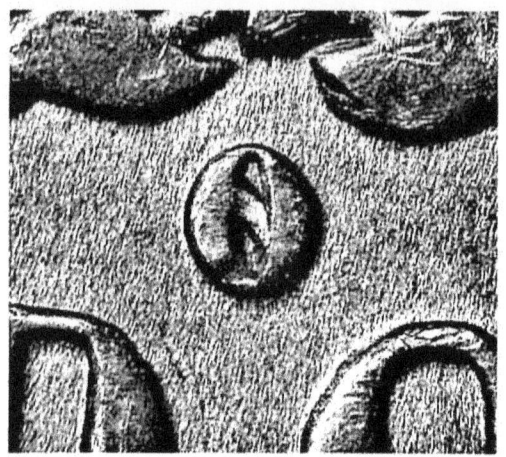

1882 O VAM 3 O/S Flush

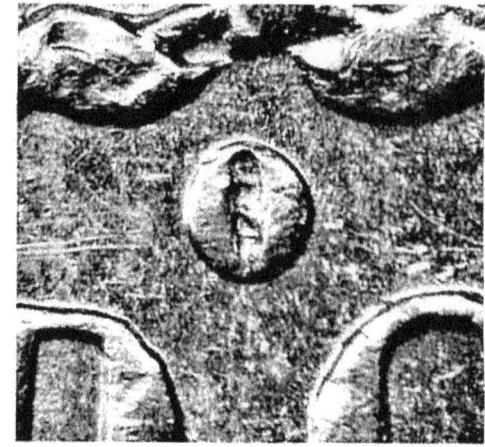

1882 O VAM 3 O/S Flush EDS

1882 O VAM 5 O/S Broken

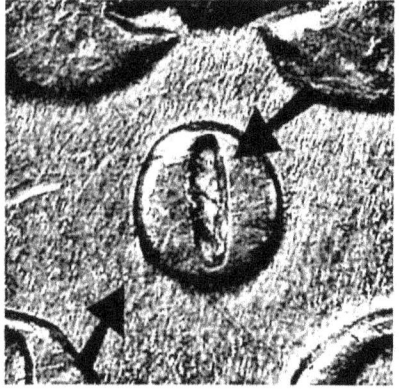

1882 O VAM 4 O/S Recessed

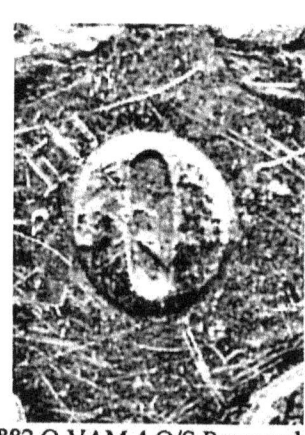

1882 O VAM 4 O/S Recessed EDS

1882 O VAM 5 O Over S Broken
EDS

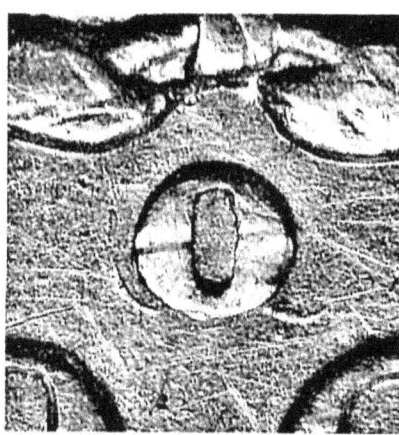

1900 O VAM 7 & 10 O/CC Low

1900 O VAM 8 O/O/CC Centered
Shifted Left

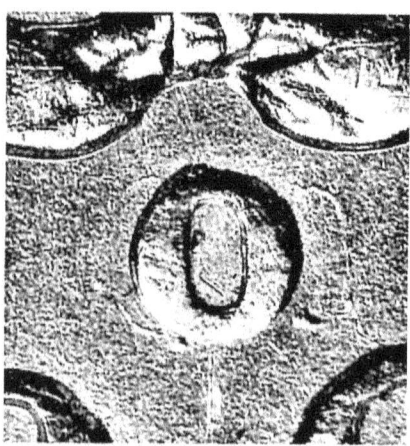

1900 O VAM 9 O/CC Center,
Shifted Right

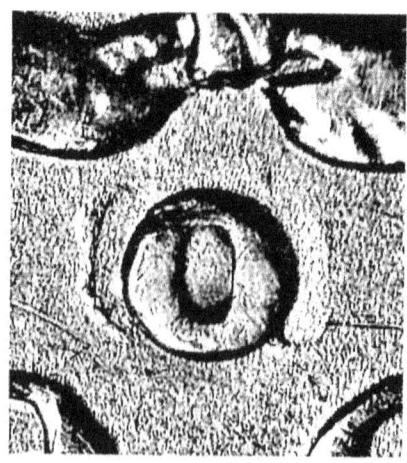

1900 O VAM 11 O/CC High,
Shifted Left

1900 O VAM 12 O/CC High,
Shifted Right

Identifying Dots

Two dates of **1884** and **1921** have **small raised dots** on coins to possibly **identify the dies**. **Two 1884 Philadelphia Mint obverse and reverse dies** have a **small raised dot alongside the designer's initial M** on the obverse at the **truncation of Liberty head** and on the **reverse** at the **wreath bow**. The width of the date and size of the date digits were slightly reduced for 1884. Possibly the dots were to identify the obverse design with **reduced date size** during the transition late in 1883 or early in 1884. It may have been used to prevent a mix up of the working hubs during the multiple hubbing of the working dies. After the transition, the raised dot on the working hub was easily ground off.

Two different size dots and positions next to the M at the bottom of the Liberty head truncation are known. The reverse dies have the same size dots but in slightly different positions next to the M on the wreath bow. It is a mystery why dots were placed on the two reverse dies since there was no design change on them in 1884. These two 1884 P dot varieties are fairly scarce and command only a modest premium.

There are also some **prominent raised dots** on several reverse working dies of the **1921 P, D & S**. The 1921 P has a fairly **large circular dot** just below the **bottom of the eagle's right wing** and another die with a **large circular dot on the field** between the bottom of the eagle's left wing and the top arrow head point. The **1921 D** has a **large circular dot** also just below the **bottom of the eagle's right wing**. Another 1921 D reverse die variety has a very small raised dot on the field above the left olive leaf cluster and several other very small raised dots on the reverse. But these dots are possibly due to trapped gas bubbles in the steel for the dies when the metal was cast. The **1921 S** has a die variety with a **very small circular raised dot between the bottom of the eagle's left wing and arrow shaft**, but this may also be due to a trapped gas bubble. There are quite a number of working dies for the 1921 Morgan and 1921 through 1924 Peace dollars that have tiny circular raised dots at various locations on the obverse and reverse dies. But they are thought to be from the gas bubbles in the steel and very few are listed as die varieties.

The two prominent large raised dots on the 1921 P and the one large dot on the 1921 D were likely deliberately punched into the working hubs to identify the **slightly different design on the later D^2 reverse working hub** when first used. Because of their large size these three dot varieties carry a modest premium.

Available references–
Top 100 Morgan Dollar Varieties: The VAM Keys, by Michael Fey & Jeff Oxman, 4th ed., 2009.

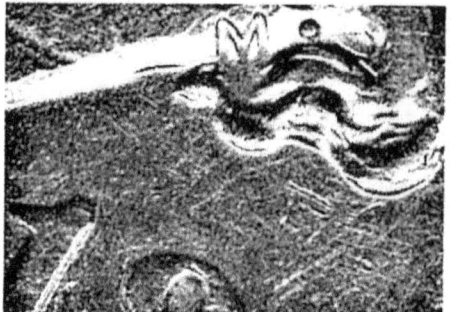

1884 P VAM 4 Small Dot

1884 P VAM 3 Large Dot

1884 P VAM 3 Dot Wreath Bow

1921 P VAM 8 Dot Wing

1921 P VAM 9 Dot Below Wing,
Gouges EDS

1921 S VAM 4 Dot Field

1921 D VAM 3 Dot Wing

1921 D VAM 4 Dot Olive Leaves

Dual Hub Dies

Dual hub working dies occurred when noticeable **different design hubs** were used in the **hubbing of particular working dies**. It was possible that different hubs were used during the seven to ten blows required to fully bring up the design on working dies. But **most cases** of dual hub dies occurred to **salvage older design fully hubbed dies**. This saved almost two weeks in the preparation of working dies since the dies could only receive one hub blow per day with annealing between each of the seven to ten hub blows. The following sub-sections treat the **five** known instances of dual hub Morgan dollar working dies.

1878 P 7 Over 8 Tail Feathers

This is the most recognized of the Morgan dollar dual hub dies with some **extra tail feather ends** protruding **below** the normal **7 tail feathers** on the eagle for the **1878 P**. It was first reported in 1948 and identified as dual hub dies in 1965. **Thirteen** dies of the first A type design with 8 tail feathers of the eagle were re-hubbed with the newer B type design hub. The A type working reverse dies cracked and sank after a short time in the coining presses. In addition, the basining of the reverse dies removed the inner wing feathers next to both legs which required time consuming **touch up engraving** to add back the missing feathers.

To save a week or two in the reverse die preparation, some reverse type **A dies were re-hubbed** with the newer **B type hub** which only took a day or two. Because there were design differences between the A and B type reverse hubs, the A type working dies had the periphery design ground off leaving the central design intact. Still there is some doubling of the central design on the re-hubbed dies, especially around the olive branch and leaves and the eagle's legs. Thirteen so-called 7 over 8 tail feather dies have been identified with some with doubled legs and 3 to 7 tail feather ends protruding below the B type seven tail feathers. They are not the usual die doubling of design shifts but one design type over another. So they are **not** called doubled tail feathers. One of the scarcest and most desirable is the **VAM 44** with 3 tail feather ends showing and strongly doubled obverse. The 7 over 8 tail feathers are highly collectable Morgan die varieties.

1878 P Doubled Eagle's Beak

An interim trial effort to salvage some early **1878 design A^1 type** reverse dies with 8 eagle's tail feathers resulted in **five reverse 1878 P** working dies being re-hubbed with the **slightly modified A^2 type** hub. This dual hub reverse was first reported in 1975. The differences between the two 8 tail feather designs was not great with improved design relief of the inner wing feathers at the leg and slight changes in the eagle's beak and location of In letters. Primary doubling of these dual hub dies occurred at the **eagle's beak**, top arrow head and top arrow shaft on the right.

1878 P Doubled LIBERTY

The **Philadelphia Mint** also had problems with the first design obverse dies. They struck only about half the average coins than the first design reverse dies. To salvage many of the **first design I type** obverse working dies, the second **obverse design II hub** was impressed into these first design working dies. No portion of the first design was first removed from these dies as the differences in the first and second obverse design were small. To date, **40 1878 P obverse** working dies have been identified as **II over I design dual hub dies**. The dual hubbing of these obverse dies was first reported in 1965.

Evidence of the dual hubbing of the 1878 P first design type I obverse working dies by a type II obverse hub shows up as frequent **doubling** of the **stars, motto letters, date and LIBERTY** in the head band. The ear also retained the characteristics of the earlier I design type with evenly divided rear portion of the ear and **pointed inner ear fill** instead of the unevenly divided rear portion and thick blunt inner ear fill of the second II design type.

Although these dual hub obverse dies don't quite have the spectacular visible flaws of the dual hub 7 over 8 tail feather dies, many are very desirable to collectors. Quite a few have strongly doubled letters, stars and date digits seldom seen on the later Morgan dollar dates. As the first year of issue, these 1878 P dual hub obverse die varieties remain very collectable. The **VAM 44** with strongly doubled obverse and 7 over 8 tail feathers is one of the more desirable and scarce dual hub varieties.

1900-1904 Two Olive Reverse

The C^3 type reverse design was used on all coins from 1881 thru 1899 and on some 1878, 1879, 1880 and 1900 thru 1903. However, the space between the eagle's neck and left wing **tended to fill up** on these dies. A slightly modified design hub of C^4 was introduced in 1900 with **larger space between the eagle's neck and left wing**, larger stars, cut down smaller olive and reduced length of the center arrow shaft. **Many dozens of the older C^3 type reverse dies** were re-impressed with the newer C^4 **type reverse hub** which showed up on some 1900 P, S; 1901 P, O, S; 1902 P, O, S; 1903 S and 1904 S.

The differences in the C^3 and C^4 designs showed up on the coins as **two olives** on the left olive branch with the top right one typically a **little shallower**. There are also various degrees of **doubling** of the **olive leaves, arrow shafts and heads, wing feathers and eagle's head**. This two olive dual hub reverse was first recognized in 1979. There is only **slight collector interest** in these dual hub varieties because of the **minor doubling** and the **many dual hub working dies** over a five years span. A few command premium prices because of the strong visible doubling, such as the **1900 P VAM 11** with strongly doubled wing feathers and arrow feathers and shafts.

1901-1904 Doubled Liberty Head Profile

There are a few isolated cases from 1878 thru 1900 of the Liberty head having a doubled profile from the forward hair edge down thru the nose, lips, chin and even the upper neck. However, beginning in **1901 thru 1904** there are **numerous examples** of **doubled** and even **some tripled profiles** of all the mints Morgan dollar coins.

In 2009 an explanation was put forth that one or more obverse hubs must have a slightly different profile size and location relative to the rest of the Liberty head. Other obverse features normally weren't doubled at the same time as the doubled profile. These doubled profiles occur in varius strengths and amounts of doubling along the vertical length of the profile. So it is not doubling on a hub which would be consistently very similar. One or more of the hubs used from 1901 thru 1904 could have had this profile location slightly shifted when the hub was made from the master die blows or even perhaps during the multiple annealing operations with new equipment at the new Philadelphia Mint that opened in 1901. These doubled profile coins are a **minor variety** and by themselves don't command much collector interest, unless they are exceptionally strong.

Available references–
1878 Morgan Dollar 8-TF Attribution Guide, by Jeff Oxman & Les Hartnett, 3rd ed., 2004.
A Guide to the Varieties of the 1878 Carson City Morgan Dollar, by John Roberts, 2010.
1878 P 7 Tail Feathers Morgan Dollar Attribution Guide, by Leroy Van Allen, Revised November 2010.
Official Guide To The 1878 Reverse of '79 Varieties, by Mark Witkower, 2008.
1878 S Morgan Dollar Attribution Guide, by Leroy Van Allen & Craig Lickenbrock, Updated March 2009.
1902 O Morgan Dollar Series Attribution Guide, by Alan Scott, 2010.
1904 O Morgan Dollar Series Attribution Guide, by Alan Scott, 2010.
Top 100 Morgan Dollar Varieties: The VAM Keys, by Michael Fey & Jeff Oxman, 4th ed., 2009.
SSDC Official Guide to the Hot 50 Morgan Dollar Varieties, by Jeff Oxman, 2000.
Official Guide to the Morgan Dollar Hit List 40, by Jeff Oxman, 2009.
Morgan Silver Dollars, by Q. David Bowers, Whitman Publishing, 2004.

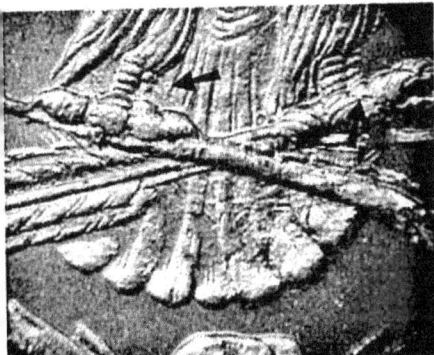

1878 P VAM 31 Doubled Legs

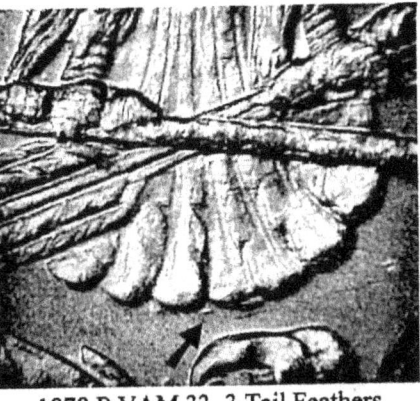

1878 P VAM 33 3 Tail Feathers

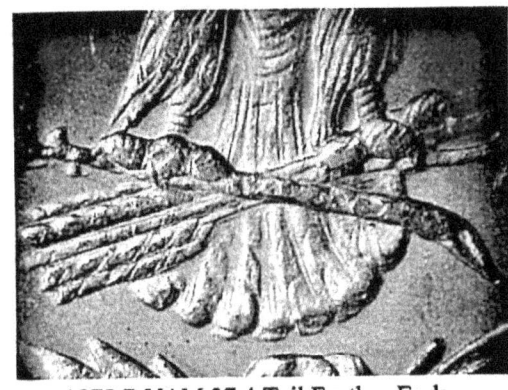

1878 P VAM 37 4 Tail Feather Ends

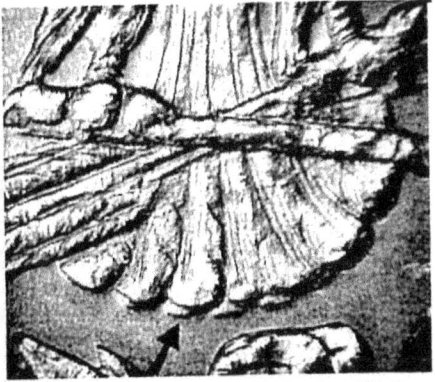

1878 P VAM 40 5 Tail Feather Ends

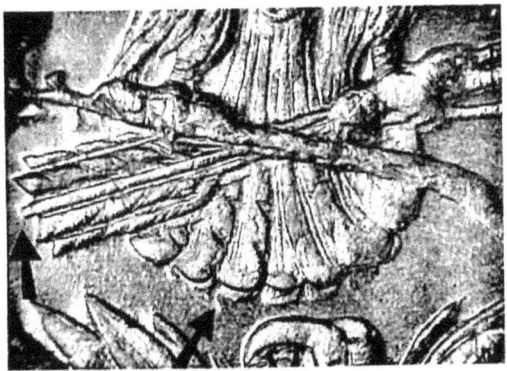

1878 P VAM 41 7 Tail Feather Ends

1878 P VAM 42 7 Tail Feather Ends

1878 P VAM 18 Doubled Olive Leaves

1878 P A² over A¹ reverse

1878 P VAM 22 Doubled Arrow Heads

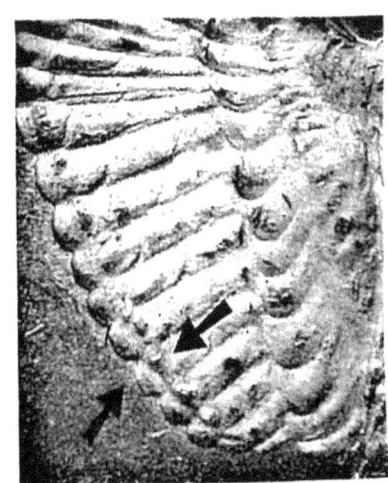

1878 P VAM 20 Doubled Wing Edge

1878 P VAM 117 Tripled Second
Right Star

1878 P VAM 142 Doubled 8-8,
Tripled 7

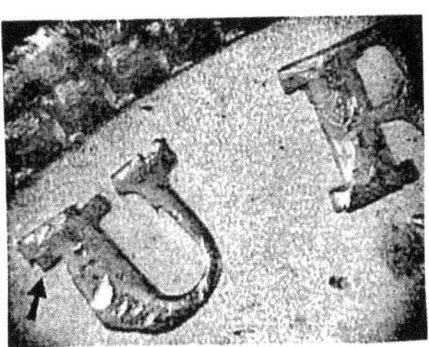

1878 P VAM 163 Shifted U

1878 P VAM 44 Doubled Obverse

1878 P VAM 82 II/I Ear

1878 P VAM 168 Doubled P

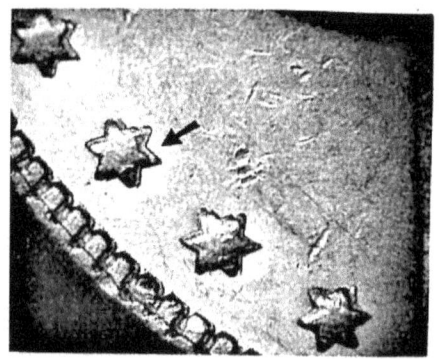

1878 P VAM 169 Quadrupled Left Stars

1878 P VAM 171 Tripled R

1878 P VAM 171 Doubled Cotton
Bolls, Cap

1900 P VAM 11 Doubled Eagle

1900 P VAM 11 Doubled Wing

1901 P VAM 22 2 Olive Reverse

1902 O VAM 61 2 Olive Reverse

1902 O VAM 74 2 Olive Reverse

1903 S VAM 6 2 Olive Reverse

 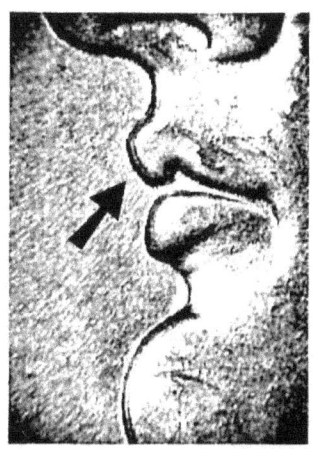 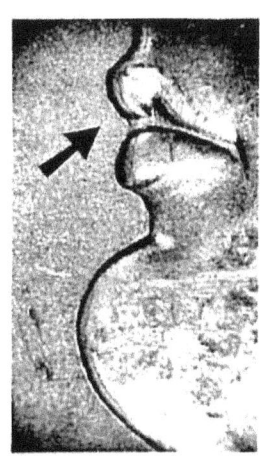 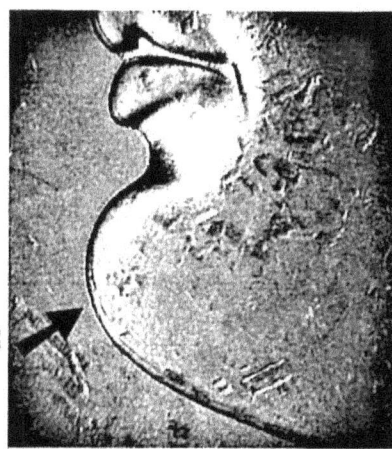

902 O VAM 21 Doubled Profile

1903 P VAM 6 Doubled Profile

1904 O VAM 12 Doubled Profile

1904 O VAM 41 Doubled Profile

Engraved Eagle's Wing Feathers

There is engraving of the feathers in the eagle's wings on many of the 1878 P & S and some 1879 S reverse working dies. This made each touched up working die **unique** since the engraving was performed by **hand** and **different**. All of the initial **A type reverse 1878 P 8 Tail Feather** working dies were touched up, some of the later **B type reverse 1878 P 7 TF** working dies, many of the **1878 S B type reverse** working dies and a few **1879 S Rev 78** working dies.

1878 P 8 Tail Feathers

The **first 8 tail feather A type reverse** working dies of the Morgan dollar were only used to strike **1878** coins at the **Philadelphia Mint.** The basining and polishing of these 8 TF working dies eliminated some of the original eagle's feathers between the lower inside of both wings and adjacent legs because this design area was too shallow on the die. This caused a **polished gap** between the lower part of **both wings and legs.** All of the known **initial 15 A type reverse working dies** were touched up by **engraving two or three short feathers** on both areas to fill the blank space with tiny feathers. In most cases the engraved feathers look fairly realistic and blend in with the other wing or leg feathers. Since all of the initial A type design working dies were touched up, this special engraving has been known since the die varieties were first listed in 1965. A couple representative examples of these engraved 8 TF dies are shown.

There are also **five 1878 P 8 TF later A type reverse working dies** with some slight differences from the initial 15 A type reverse working dies. They are characterized by a doubled eagle's lower beak, hooked upper beak and I of In is away from the eagle's wing. A couple of these dies show slight remnants of an underlying engraved wing feathers from dual hubbing of the later 8 TF design over an earlier type 8 TF working die that already had engraved feathers added.

1878 P 7 Tail Feathers

The various mints experienced difficulties in **1878** in the basining and polishing the **second B type reverse** with **7 TF and flat eagle's breast.** The middle of the eagle's wings and bottom feather next to the eagle's right leg were frequently over polished with weak or missing feathers because of the low relief of the working dies in these areas. The **Philadelphia Mint** touched up **seven** of these over polished working dies at the **eagle's right wing and leg.** The strongest and first reported **1878 P 7 TF** touched-up feathers is the **VAM 189** reported in 2002 as shown in the accompanying photograph with some diagonal lines engraved at the wing-leg junction. The other six engraved dies have small and shallow vertical bars and lines in the over polished area that hardly resemble the missing feathers. Also, there are **five 1878 P of B type reverse** working dies first reported in 2007 that show small **engraved bars and lines** at the **junction of the eagle's right wing and body** that frequently had a wide gap from over polishing.

1878 S

Touched up engraving on the **1878 S** working dies at the **eagle's right wing and leg** was first reported in 1979. Since then, **41** of the **1878 S** reverse working dies have been identified with this touch up engraving with four of these dies being acid treated as discussed in a separate section, **Acid Treated Dies.** Most of these engraved feathers are raised and smooth that blend into the adjacent feathers to look realistic. A sampling of these engraved feathers for the 1878 S is shown in the accompanying photographs. In addition, **seven reverse dies** were touched-up in the **middle of the eagle's wings** in an attempt to fill in missing feathers and **17** had the **engraved lines** extend up to the eagle's right **wing-body junction.** The 1878 CC reverse working dies weren't touched up, so the many 1878 S touched up reverse dies is a **unique** example of a branch mint doing extensive heavy engraving on many working dies.

1879 S

In addition, **six 1879 S Rev 78 working dies** also have touched up **engraved wing-leg feathers.** Two of these, 1879 S VAM 9 with the same 1878 S reverse die of VAM 45 and 1879 S VAM 4 with the same 1878 S reverse die of VAM 1C, were used to strike coins in these two different years. These 1879 S Rev 78 working dies with engraved wing-leg feather were likely engraved in 1878 and were left over reverse dies used the next year in 1879.

Available references–
1878 Morgan Dollar 8-TF Attribution Guide, by Jeff Oxman & Les Hartnett, 3rd ed., 2004.
Morgan Dollar 8 & 7 Over 8 Tail Feather Story, by Leroy Van Allen, revised January 2006.
1878 P 7 Tail Feathers Morgan Dollar Attribution Guide, by Leroy Van Allen, Revised November 2010.
1878 S Morgan Dollar Attribution Guide, by Leroy Van Allen & Craig Lickenbrock, Updated March 2009.
A "Retouching" Story, by Leroy Van Allen, *Numismatist*, June 2007.
Top 100 Morgan Dollar Varieties: The VAM Keys, by Michael Fey & Jeff Oxman, 4th ed., 2009.
SSDC Official Guide to the Hot 50 Morgan Dollar Varieties, by Jeff Oxman, 2000.
Official Guide To The Morgan Dollar Hit List 40, by Jeff Oxman, 2009.

1878 P VAM 1 Engraved Wing Feathers

1878 P VAM 5 Engraved Wing Feathers

1878 P VAM 7 Engraved Wing Feathers

1878 P VAM 9 Engraved Wing Feathers

1878 P VAM 14-1 Engraved Wing Feathers

1878 P VAM 18 Wing Feathers

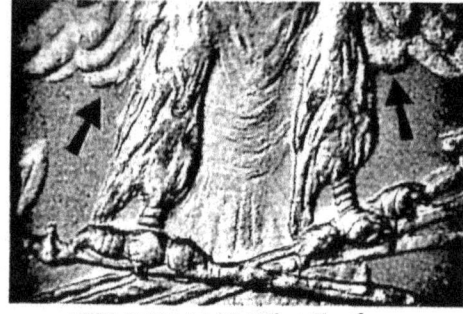

1878 P VAM 19 Wing Feathers

1878 P VAM 22 Engraved Wing Feathers

1878 P VAM 189 Engraved Wing Feathers

1878 P VAM 189 Engraved Wing Feathers

1878 P VAM 123 Engraved Wing Feather

1878 P VAM 141 Engraved Wing Feather

1878 P VAM 165 Diagonal Engraved Wing Bars

1878 P VAM 168 Engraved Bars

1878 S VAM 1 Normal Wing
Feather

1878 S VAM 22 Over Polished
Wing-Leg

1878 S VAM 6 Engraved Wing
Feather

1878 S VAM 8 Engraved Wing Feather

1878 S VAM 20 Engraved Wing Feather

1878 S VAM 38 Engraved Wing
Feather

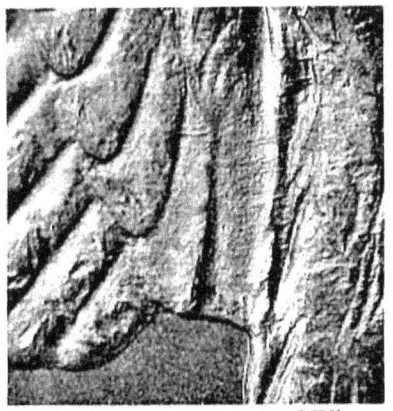

1878 S VAM 45 Engraved Wing
Feather

1878 S VAM 64 Engraved Wing
Feather With Lines

1878 S VAM 69 Engraved Wing
Feather

1879 S Rev 78 VAM 6 Engraved
Wing Feather

1878 S Rev 78 VAM 9 Engraved Wing
Feather

1878 S VAM 18 Lines in Wing

1878 S VAM 18 Lines in Wing

1878 S VAM 6 Engraving on Feathers

1878 S VAM 6 Engraving Lines

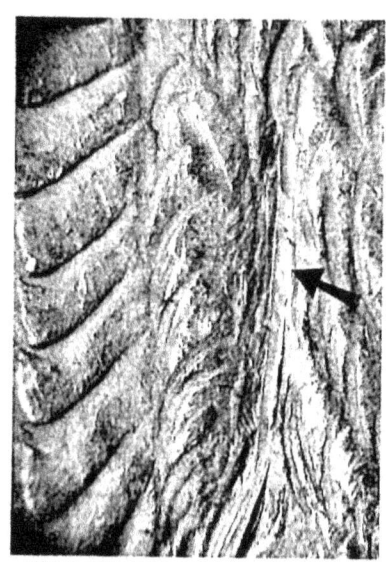

1878 S VAM 8 Engraving Lines

1878 S VAM 21 Engraving
Wing-Body, Gouge

1878 S VAM 53 Engraving Wing-Body

8 & 9 Upper Tail Feathers

Only recently in May 2010 and July 2011 was it discovered that the San Francisco Mint workman had added an **engraved 8ᵗʰ and 9ᵗʰ upper tail feather** to two **1878 S** and two **1879 S** Morgan dollar reverse dies and **strengthened** two of these upper tail feathers on a third die of **1879 S**. Two of these dies were of the normal B^2 type reverse design and one of the later C type design, both with a **normal seven tail feathers** above and below the olive branch and arrow shafts.

The working dies of the B^2 type design frequently had portions of the shallow design removed when the dies were basined at the Philadelphia, Carson City and San Francisco Mints. The lower feather of the eagle's right wing next to the leg would become weak or missing altogether and were touched up by engraving back a feather there on some Philadelphia Mint working dies and many San Francisco Mint working dies as discussed a separate section on **Engraved Eagle's Wing Feathers**. Also, the far left upper tail feather would frequently become very shallow or with portions missing next to the eagle's claw for the B^2 type reverse and sometimes on the C type reverse. This is shown in the accompanying photographs comparing a B^2 type normal full upper 7 tail feather (Count the tops of the upper tail feathers.) with an over polished left upper tail feather. The Philadelphia and Carson City Mints didn't perform engraving on these B^2 design upper tail feathers. However, the San Francisco Mint engraved at these upper tail feathers on two known B^2 type reverse dies and one C type reverse die.

Strengthened Engraved Upper Tail Feather

The **first reported engraving on an upper tail feathers** was reported in early May 2010 for a C type reverse on a **1879 S VAM 74** with **strengthened** far left two tail feathers as shown in the accompany photograph. This is compared to a normal full upper tail feathers for C type reverse and also compared to one that is a typical over polished upper tail feather. The left engraved feather is further left and wider than normal and both engraved feathers have horizontal engraving lines for some unknown reason.

Added 8ᵗʰ & 9ᵗʰ Engraved Upper Tail Feather

In late May 2010, **two added engraved far left upper tail feathers** on the B^2 type reverse were reported as shown in the accompanying photograph to make a total of **9 upper tail feathers**. Actually these two added tail feather bars are mostly in a normally blank space at the far left upper tail feathers. Why the added two tail feathers were engraved so far left is a mystery– perhaps the workman mistakenly thought this was an over polished area. This particular die was used for two **1878 S VAMs 45 & 68** varieties and then **again in 1879 S for VAMs 9 & 77**, an **unusual** confirmed case of a reverse die being used in two different years for the Morgan dollar.

Added 8ᵗʰ Engraved Upper Tail Feather

The die with the 9 upper tail feather was **later polished** removing the engraved left upper tail feather and made the right extra tail feather a thin sliver and the two left normal upper tail feathers thin and shallow as shown in the accompanying photograph. It is designated **1879 S VAM 77A** with **8** upper tail feathers.

A **more recent case** reported in July 2011 of engraving an **8ᵗʰ upper tail feather** on a B^2 type reverse is shown in the accompany photograph. A wide and high vertical bar was engraved to the left of the normal far left upper tail feather to make a total of **8 upper tail feathers** on an **1878 S VAM 110**. This reverse die is also shared with the 1878 S VAM 64 and has an engraved wing feather with **unusual** horizontal engraved lines on it on the eagle's right wing next to the leg.

Summary

The **San Francisco Mint** performed some **unique engraving** on the **upper tail feathers** of the eagle that the other mints never engraved. One **1879 S** die shows engraving to **strengthen two left normal upper tail feathers**, another die used in 1878 and again in 1879 shows **two added engraved upper tail feathers** for a total of **9** with the die later polished to show only **8 upper tail feathers**, and a third die of **1878** shows **one added engraved upper tail feather** for a total of **8**.

Available references–

1878 S Morgan Dollar Attribution Guide, by Leroy Van Allen & Craig Lickenbrock, updated
March 2009.

A Guide To The 1879-S Reverse of 1878 Morgan Silver Dollars, by David Wang, 2001.

1879 S VAM 75 Typical Over Polished
Tail Feathers

1879 S VAM 2 Normal Full Tail Feathers

1879 S VAM 74 Engraved Tail Feathers

1879 S Rev 78 VAM 9 Two Engraved
Extra Tail Feathers

1879 S Rev 78 VAM 77 Two Engraved
Extra Tail Feathers

1879 S Rev 78 VAM 77A Polished
Engraved 8 Tail Feathers

1879 S Rev 78 VAM 42 Over Polished
Upper Tail Feathers

1878 CC VAM 9 Full Upper Tail Feathers

1878 S VAM 110 Engraved 8th Upper Tail Feathers

1878 S VAM 110 Engraved Wing
Feather With Lines

Engraved Liberty Head

There are many reverse dies that have had lower wing feathers engraved back in the over polished area at the eagle's lower wing-leg junction for the 1878 P 8TF, 1878 P 7TF, 1878 S and 1879 S Rev 78 years. However, the Morgan dollar series **only has two known cases of engraving on the obverse dies**. One is the **1878 S VAM 29/31** with **engraving at the jaw line** to remove die doubling there. The other known example is an **1904 O VAM 41/44** that also has **fine engraving along the jaw** and **upper neck edge** to remove die doubling there. Some 1921 Morgan dollars have fine scribbling die scratches on the upper jaw area but not the heavy engraved lines of the 1878 S and 1904 O.

In 2003 it was reported that an 1878 S had an unusual 'sagging jaw' line. At the time, it was thought this was die doubling since the nostril and eyelid were strongly doubled. But in 2006 an nice uncirculated specimen was examined and it was discovered that this VAM 29/31 die variety had many engraved parallel lines at the jaw edge. So this was a case of the San Francisco Mint performing crude engraving on the obverse die jaw edge cavity to remove some obvious strong die doubling there. The engraving resulted is a somewhat distorted drooping jaw line dubbed **Sagging Jaw**.

Another similar case of engraving on a doubled jaw line was reported in 2009 for the 1904 O VAM 41/44. The parallel engraved lines along the jaw edge and upper neck edge was done to erase the strong doubling on the die. But the die engraving in this case didn't significantly distort the shape of the jaw line.

Usually uncirculated coin examples are needed to clearly see the engraving lines on both of these **unusual** examples of **engraving on the obverse dies** by **branch mints**.

Available references–
1878 S Morgan Dollar Attribution Guide, by Leroy Van Allen & Craig Lickenbrock, Updated March 2009.
1904 O Morgan Dollar Series Attribution Guide, by Alan Scott, 2010.

1878 S VAM 51 Normal Jaw

1878 S VAM 29 Engraved Jaw
Sagging Jaw

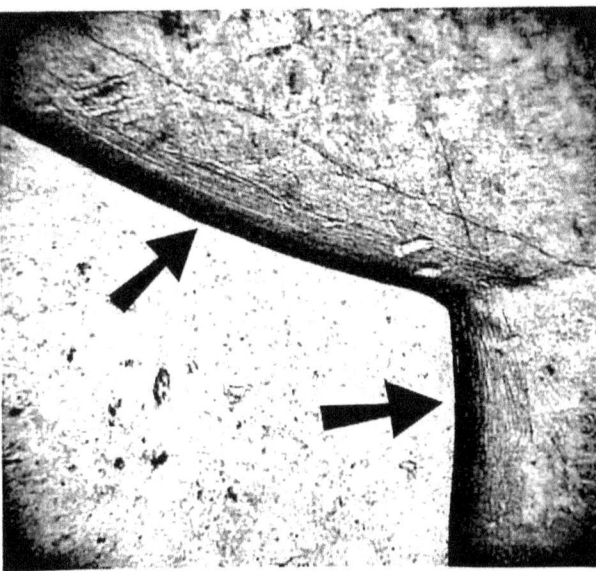
1904 O VAM 41 Engraved Jaw & Neck

1878 S VAM 29 Die File Lines Jaw

Acid Treated Dies

Acid treated dies that **etched away part of the die surfaces** are known only for some **1878 S, 1879 S** and **1882 S** die varieties. It was an **unauthorized practice only performed at the San Francisco Mint** for these three years. Use of acid was an attempt to **repair and fill in over polished areas** on some of the obverse and reverse dies of those three years.

The mints had problems with basining and polishing the early Morgan dollar obverse and reverse dies. Sometimes the **lower hair edge** of the **obverse** Liberty head would be over polished with **wide missing hair gaps**. On the **reverse** dies, often the **feathers at the eagle's right leg and wing** junction would be polished very **shallow** or **missing** on the **second B type reverse** dies as well as the **middle** of the **wings**. These design areas were strengthened on the later **C type reverse**, but often the **left wreath leaves** would become shallow or disconnected from the die over polishing.

To repair some of the 1878 S and 1879 S over polished B type reverse dies, the San Francisco Mint **engraved by hand** a **feather between the eagle's right wing and leg** that somewhat resembled the missing feather on **41** of the **1878 S reverse dies** and **six** of the **1879 S reverse dies. Four** of the **1878 S reverse dies** had different and **strange smooth or dotted surfaces** dubbed **"funky feathers"**. The earliest of these were reported by Pete Bishal in July 1981 and Martin Field in August 1981. At that time, they were thought to be crude examples of die engraving using traditional engraver's tools.

It wasn't until September 2010 that Brian Raines reported an 1879 S obverse that he said had been severely polished at the lower hair edge, but filled back in, possibly with acid like one of the 1878 S funky feathers. The **key** to identify acid treated areas or etching is the **flat raised smooth surface** with **sharp ragged edges** and sometimes **tiny raised dots**. Normal die polishing doesn't leave well defined raised areas with sharp edges on coins. After the reporting of an acid treated obverse by Brian Raines, a number of other obverse and reverse dies of 1878 S, 1879 S and 1882 S have since been identified as being acid treated.

The San Francisco Mint refined bullion for many years including 1878 and 1879. **Nitric acid** was used to extract and refine the silver from the gold and silver granulations made from the bullion deposited at the mints. Nitric acid dissolved the silver in the bullion as chloride of silver and **sulfuric acid** was used to aid the reduction of the chloride by zinc to extract the pure silver. It is not known whether nitric or sulfuric acid was used on a particular die or the concentration and length of time left to etch the steel surface. The San Francisco Mint workers likely experimented with the two acid types with varying strengths and duration on the die face that produced different results.

Those four 1878 S funky feathers have two with smooth tops and sharp edges to the added **wing-leg junction feather** typical of an acid treated surface. However, two other 1878 S funky feathers have flat surfaces and sharp ragged edges but with numerous raised dots and splotches of a more violent acid reaction. Other acid treated areas to strengthen over polished design areas include the **wing middle and upper tail feathers** for an 1878 S, **left wreath leaves** of 1879 S and 1882 S and the **lower obverse hair edges** of 1878 and 1879 S.

It is currently known that the San Francisco Mint performed unauthorized die modification using nitric and/or sulfuric acid on **one 1878 S obverse die** and **six reverse dies, two 1879 S obverse dies** and **two reverse dies** and **one 1882 S reverse die** in an attempt to fill in flat over polished areas on the die surfaces. No other mints using Morgan dollar dies performed this **unusual** die repair procedure. It was of limited success because the resulting ragged edges and smooth flat surfaces were not typical of over polished and missing hair edges or more rounded feathers. An **amazing** case of **unauthorized** die modification by a **branch mint** during three years!

Available references–

1878 S Morgan Dollar Attribution Guide, by Leroy Van Allen & Craig Lickenbrock, Updated
      March 2009.
Official Guide to the Morgan Dollar Hit List 40, by Jeff Oxman, 2009.

1878 S VAM 36 Acid Treated Splotches

1878 S VAM 36 Acid Treated Splotches

1878 S VAM 36 Acid Treated Streaks

1878 S VAM 49 Acid Treated Area

1878 S VAM 50 Acid Treated Area & Dots

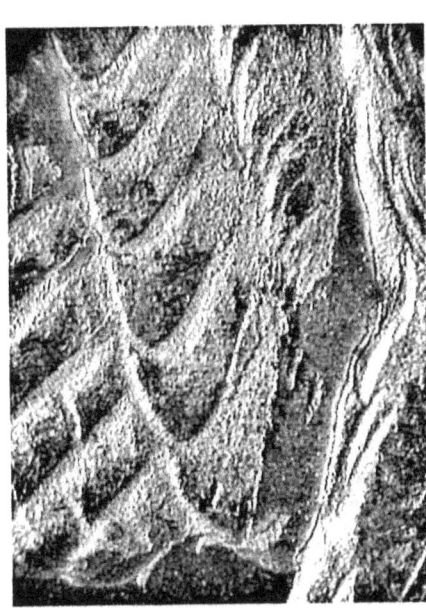

1878 S VAM 76 Acid Treated Area

1878 S VAM 81 Acid Treated Areas & Dots

1878 S VAM 55 Acid Treated Streaks

1878 S VAM 78 Acid Treated Hair Areas

1879 S VAM 1E Acid Treated Hair Areas

1879 S VAM 1E Acid Treated Lower Hair Right Vee

1879 S VAM 45 Acid Treated Wreath Leaves

1879 S VAM 64 Acid Treated Hair Edge

1879 S VAM 78 Acid Treated Leaf Cluster

1879 S VAM 78 Acid Treated Leaves

1882 S VAM 3 Acid Treated Left Wreath Leaves

1882 S VAM 3 Acid Treated Right Wreath Leaves

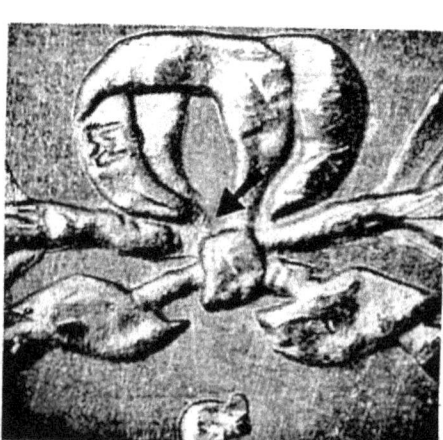

1882 S VAM 3 Acid Treated Left Stem

1921 Scribbles

Scribbles on the **1921 Morgan dollar reverse working dies** are very fine die scratches in various directions around the eagle's right leg, the **junction of the eagle's left wing and body, middle of the wings** and sometimes on the **Liberty head face**. The mint workers at the Philadelphia, San Francisco and Denver Mints touched up these areas on **hundreds of 1921 working dies** that had **missing** and **flat feather detail** from the basining and polishing of the reverse dies. Sharp pointed engraving tools and stones were likely used at the mints to touch-up the hardened working dies.

These scribbling die scratches were a **half-hearte**d and **quick** attempt to repair over polished dies since it takes a 10X or better hand magnifying glass to detect the fine scratch lines. The **shallow** and **fine** die scratches **hardly resemble** the two **rounded upper tail feathers** at the leg that were weakened or removed by the die polishing. They only provide a **dull finish** on the over polished area to the naked eye.

Since the scribbles were put on the working dies **by hand** by the mint workman at each mint, they have an importance as **repaired dies by the mints** and therefore as **collectible die varieties**. Each repaired die has a **unique scribbles pattern** that can be **useful to identify the dies**. To date, well over **150 1921 Philadelphia** reverse dies have been listed with scribbles with about one-third being the early D^1 type reverse and the rest the later D^2 type reverse. Roughly half of the D^1 reverse dies seem to have scribbles with 80- 90% of the D^2 type reverse dies have scribbles. Over **100 1921 D** reverse dies with scribbles have been listed with around 90% of the 1921 D dies seem to have scribbles. The **1921 S** only have around **40** reverse dies with scribbles listed with about one-third of the 1921 S dies seem to have scribbles.

Scribble, according to the dictionary, is to write **hastily** and **carelessly** without regard to legibility or form or to cover with **careless** or **worthless** writings or drawings. These fine lines in various directions are different for each die and certainly qualify as scribbles. They don't resemble the missing feathers, are invisible to the naked eye except as a dulling of the area and they fade away from die wear. They are not like the engraved wing feathers put back on the 1878 P and S dies.

Scribbles at the 1921 Morgan dollar eagle's right leg was only recently discovered in 2006 and at the eagle's left wing and body junction and middle of the wings in 2007. The scribbles on the jaw of the Liberty head was reported in 2008.

Typical examples of the full and over polished leg and wing areas are shown in the accompanying photographs for a 1921 P and S. Some of the many different scribble patterns are shown in the photographs.

Available references–
1921 Scribbles Morgan Dollar Attribution Guide, by Leroy Van Allen and Crae Morton, November
2008.

1921 P VAM 1 Fully Struck Leg Area

1921 P VAM 1 Fully Struck Wing

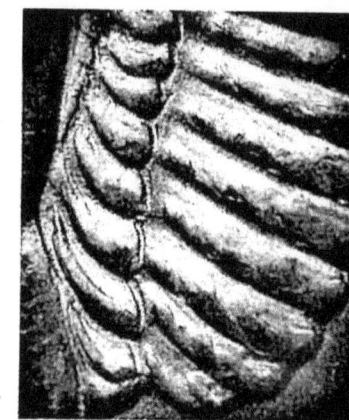

1921 P VAM 1 Fully Struck Wing

1921 S VAM 1 Over Polished Leg Area

1921 S VAM 1L Over Polished Wing

1921 S VAM 1L Over Polished Wing

1921 P VAM 3F1 Scribbling Die Scratches

1921 P VAM 3BR Scribbling Die Scratches

1921 P VAM 3CT Scribbling Die Scratches

1 1921 P VAM 3DV Scribbling Die Scratches

1921 P VAM 3DC Scribbling Die Scratches

1921 P VAM 78 Scribbling Die Scratches

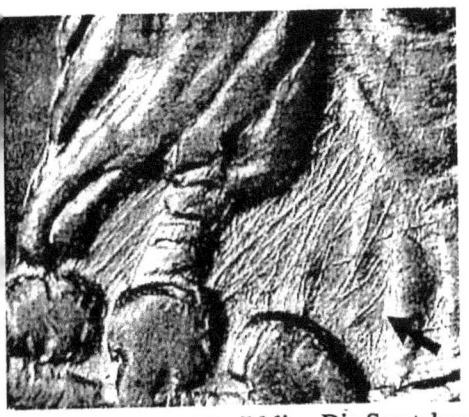

1921 D VAM 1M Scribbling Die Scratches

1921 D VAM 1U Scribbling Die Scratches

1921 D VAM 1BU Scribbling Die Scratches

1921 D VAM 1CB Scribbling Die Scratches

1921 D VAM 1CC Scribbling Die Scratches

1921 D VAM 1CD Scribbling Die Scratches

1921 S VAM 1AA1 Scribbling Die Scratches

1921 S VAM 1AW Scribbling Die Scratches

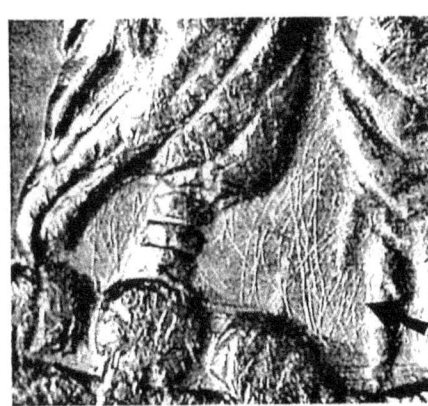

1921 S VAM 1BG Scribbling Die Scratches

1921 P VAM 36 Scribbling Die Scratches Jaw

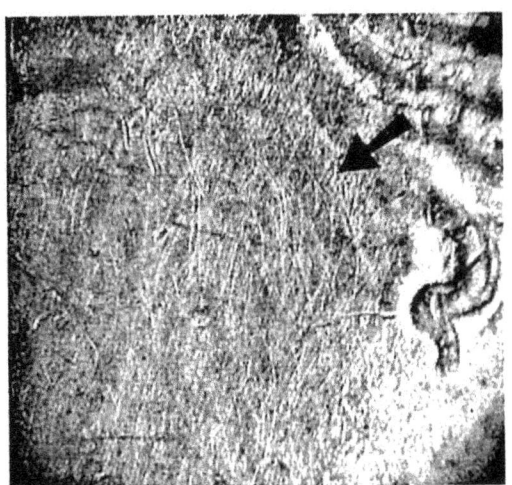

1921 P VAM 3ER Scribbling Die Scratches Cheek

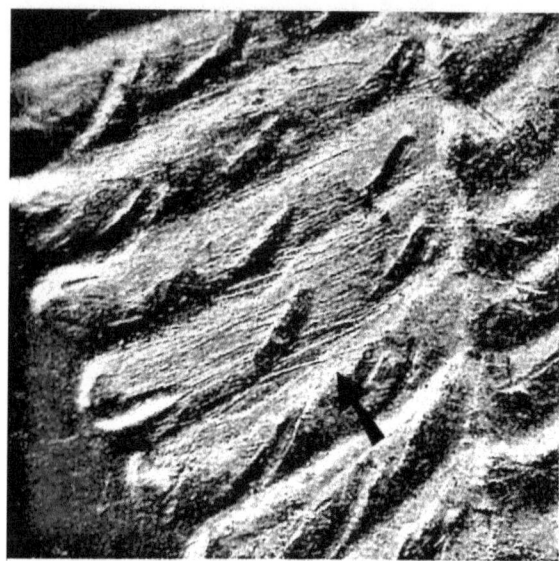

1921 P VAM 3DV Scribbling Wing Middle

1921 P VAM 3BB Scribbling Wing Middle

1921 P VAM 3EM Scribbling Wing Middle

1921 D VAM 1CD Scribbling Wing Middle

Die Polishing and 'File' Lines

Die polishing and die file lines on coins indicate an attempt by mint workers, usually the die set-up workers or supervisor for the Morgan dollars, to repair the dies that had obvious die clash marks, cracks, gouges, rust pitting or other die flaws. These die repairs may have been performed on the dies while still in the coining press or on them when they had been removed. The repairs resulted in fine lines in the fields and sometimes in the depth of the design on the die.

It differs from the initial die polishing and buffing which generally left mirror-like fields with perhaps only isolated faint polishing lines in the fields. But the initial die polishing often left fine parallel lines in the devices high points on the die, such as in the hair and LIBERTY letters on the obverse and the wreath and bow plus eagle's feathers on the reverse. These initial polishing lines in the devices were seldom very visible to the naked eye however, and generally aren't listed as die varieties.

The repair of dies thru polishing was generally more visible with coarser lines on small patches. Fine emery cloth on a stick to create a flat surface was sometimes rubbed against a die face while the die was still in the press in an attempt to erase the die flaws. Die clash marks were the most common flaw worked on. Because of the limited frontal access to the dies while still in a coining press, the polishing lines would usually be at about the vertical direction on the die face because of the back and forth motion of the hand held emery cloth stick by a workman. If the flawed die had been removed from the coining press, then the polishing lines could occur in any direction.

The coarser repair lines on a die are commonly called die file lines. In reality a conventional metal file wouldn't be very effective in removing flaws on the hardened working die face and would only produce perhaps some isolated scratches. Fine emery cloth would produce fine parallel lines over a wide area and could remove the die metal over a flat area. An abrasive stone may also have been used and would have produced more randomly spaced lines in various directions which is sometimes seen on coins.

One of the earliest reported cases in 1982 of excessive die file lines is the 1921 P VAM 1B with heavy lines all over the reverse fields. Many of the 1878 P 8 & 7 TF reverse dies have heavy isolated die polishing lines in the fields. An example is the 1878 P 7TF VAM 134 with lines at ONE on the reverse die. An example of heavy polishing lines in one area is the 1882 S VAM 18. A heavily polished obverse die is the 1880 S VAM 16A. Another 1880 S VAM 70 has heavy polishing lines on the reverse. The 1891 S VAM 5D has heavy polishing lines on the obverse and reverse. There is heavy polishing lines in the wheat leaves of the 1900 O VAM 2A. A good example of die file lines at a clash mark is the 1921 P VAM 3BK2. Heavy die file lines on the Liberty forehead shows on the 1921 P VAM 3AM. The 1921 S VAM 13A has heavy die file lines on the left and right reverse fields. There is heavy die file lines at the date of the 1921 S VAM 1X. Additional heavy die polishing examples are shown in the accompanying photographs.

Available references–
1878 P 7 Tail Feathers Morgan Dollar Attribution Guide, by Leroy Van Allen, Revised November 2010.

1878 P VAM 134 Polishing Lines

1880 S VAM 16A Polished Obverse

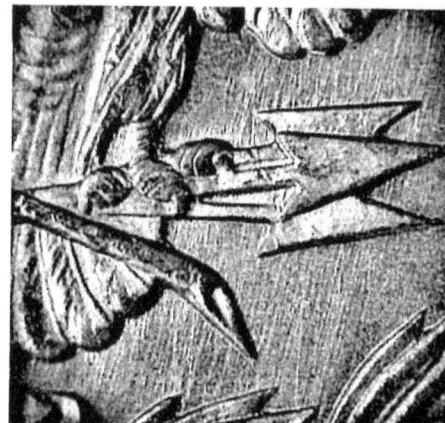

1880 S VAM 70 Polishing Lines Reverse

1882 S VAM 18 Polishing Lines

1891 S VAM 5B Polished Obverse

1891 S VAM 5D Polishing Lines

1900 O VAM 2A Polishing
Lines Wheat Stalks

1921 P VAM 1B Die File Lines

1921 P VAM 3AM Die File Lines
Forehead

1921 P VAM 3BK2 Die File Lines,
Double Clash Marks

1921 S VAM 1X Die File Lines

1921 S VAM 13A Die File Lines

1879 S VAM 11A Die File Lines

1880 S VAM 19A Polishing Lines

1891 S VAM 15 Reverse Polishing Lines

1900 P VAM 5A Polishing Lines

1900 P VAM 5A Polishing Lines

1903 P VAM 1A Die File Lines

1903 P VAM 1A Die File Lines

1921 P VAM 1J Polished Middle Reverse

1921 P VAM 1M Die File Lines

1921 P VAM 31A Die File Lines Reverse

1921 P VAM 81A Lines Wing Middle

1921 P VAM 1G Polished Upper Reverse

1921 S VAM 1H Die File Lines

1921 S VAM 1W Die File Lines

1921 S VAM 1AD Die File Lines

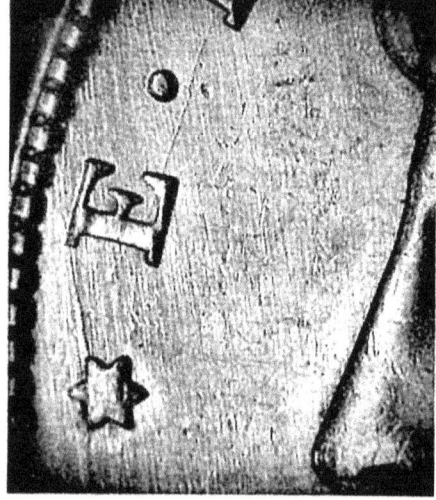

1921 S VAM 1AB Die File Lines

1921 S VAM 1AP2 Die File Lines Neck

1921 S VAM 1AF Die File Lines

1921 S VAM 1AL Die File Lines

1921 S VAM 2A Die File Lines

1921 S VAM 1BR Die File Lines

Edge Reeding

Most collectors don't give the edge of the Morgan dollar coin a second thought and seldom examine it. The edge reeding of ridges and valleys looks about the same on all of the coins. But there are some *surprising* things about the Morgan dollar edge reeding!

The edge reeding on a coin was produced on the Morgan dollars by a flat circular steel plate, called a **collar**, with a center hole of nominal 1.5 inch diameter. This hole had groves in the side that imparted the ridges and valleys on the coin edge when it was struck. All collars were initially made in 1878 at the Philadelphia Mint and shipped to the branch mints along with the obverse and reverse die pairs. Apparently later in 1878 and the following years, each mint made their own collars to fit the different dimensions of the assortment of coining presses used at the various mints. This resulted in different edge reeding counts at the mints that struck the Morgan dollar.

To produce the groves on the hole edge of the collar, a slightly tapered cylinder, or **reeding tool**, with groves on the surface was used. A milling machine made the grooves on the cylinder. The operator would set the indexing space on the milling machine to give a certain number of grooves around this reeding or swaging tool. The reeding tool was forced into the collar hole to produce the collar ridges and valleys of the reeding that made a certain number of reeding on the coin edge when struck in a coining press.

There are surprising trends in the edge reeding count for the coins struck at the Philadelphia and branch mints. Generally, the reeding count for the **Carson City Mint** struck coins is **177 or 178**. Those struck by the **New Orleans Mint** are **176** reeds for 1879- 1882 and **181** for 1882 thru 1904 and some with 188, 189 and 190 for 1899 thru 1904. The **San Francisco Mint** coins **vary widely** from **179** to **189** for 1878 thru 1882 and then **184 to 191** for 1883 thru 1900 and **189** from 1901 thru 1904. The **Philadelphia Mint** reeding counts also **varied widely** from **168 to 194** in 1878, **178 to 181** for 1879 thru 1883, **188 to 193** for 1883, **187 to 190** from 1884 thru 1900 and **189** for 1901 thru 1904. **Proof coins** struck at the Philadelphia Mint had reeding of **179** from 1879 thru 1894, **188 to 190** for 1895 thru 1899 and **186** for 1900 thru 1904. All Morgan dollar coins struck during **1921** had a **standardized 189** edge reeding with the exception discussed later of one low count collar used to strike some coins at the Philadelphia Mint.

Generally the **Carson City Mint** coins have **unique reeding count** of 177 or 178 for all years struck. The **New Orleans Mint** coins have **unique count** of **181** for the years 1884- 1904. **Proof** coins have **unique counts** of 179 for 1883-1894 and 186 for 1900- 1904. The **San Francisco Mint** had some unique counts of **182-187** for the years of 1878- 1882 and **184- 187** from 1883- 1895. The **Philadelphia Mint** had some **unique counts** of **180** from 1878- 1883, **188 and 189** from 1883- 1886 and **189 and 190** from 1887-1889 and **189** from 1893- 1894.

There are two exceptions known that fall outside the usual reeding count range of 176 to 194 for the Morgan dollar. The **lowest reeding count of 157** for the **1921 P** was first reported by Dr. William Q. Wolfson and discussed in the December 23, 1964 issue of *Coin World* in James G. Johnson's **Fair to Very Fine** column. Wolfson called it "**Infrequent Reeded**" or I. R., although "**wide reeding**" has been used recently as a simpler designation. Wolfson had also first reported the second lowest reeding count of **168** for a single **1878 P** variety with the later C type reverse early in 1965 in a summary report of the 1921 P I.R. The 1921 P has seven die pair varieties with an early D^1 type reverse and 157 reeding plus one die pair with the later D^2 type reverse.

To **check the edge reeding count** on a Morgan dollar, the most obvious way is to visually go around the edge to obtain a total count, or alternatively, mark off every 10 reeds with a fine lead pencil and sum the total. This can be quite tedious and time consuming. Another way is to make a permanent impression on paper thru a piece of carbon paper by rolling the coin edge from a starting point and back. This also requires counting a large number of impressions that is time consuming.

The **quickest, easiest and most accurate way**, however, is to use a silver dollar of known reeding count, such as a New Orleans coin from 1883 thru 1898 with 181 reeds or a 1921 Morgan dollar or any Peace dollar with 189 reeds. The unknown and known reeding coins are then held together locking the reeding together and rotated like gears back to the starting index such as the date 1 on both coins. The index point of the known coin can then be slid back or forth to the unknown index point to give an addition or subtraction to the known count for the correct count of the unknown coin. Once practiced a few times, the accurate reeding count can be obtained in a couple of seconds.

Available references–

1921 P Infrequently Reeded or Wide Reeding Morgan Dollar Attribution Guide, revised January 2009.
1878 P 7 Tail Feathers Morgan Dollar Attribution Guide, by Leroy Van Allen, Revised November 2010.
Official Guide To The 1878 Reverse of '79 Varieties, by Mark Witkower, 2008.
Top 100 Morgan Dollar Varieties: The VAM Keys, by Michael Fey & Jeff Oxman, 4th ed., 2009.
Official Guide to the Morgan Dollar Hit List 40, by Jeff Oxman, 2009.

YEAR	157	168	176	177	178	179	180	181	182	183	184	185	186	187	188	189	190	191	192	193	194
1878		F	P	P CC	CC P	P CC	P	S			S	S	S		Pr P	Pr P				Pr P	P
79			O	CC	CC P	Pr P S	P	P S	S	S	S	S									P
80			O	CC	CC P	Pr P	P	P	S	S	S	S	S	S	P S	S					
81			O		CC	Pr P	P	P	S	S	S	S	S	S		S					
82		P O		CC	CC P	Pr P	P	P O		S		S	S	S							
83					CC		P	P O					S	S	P				P	P	
84				CC	CC			O						P S	P	P					
85			O	CC		Pr		O				S			S	P	P				
86						Pr		O							S	P	P	P			
87								O				S	S	S		P	P				
88								O					S	S	S	P	P	P			
89				CC		Pr		O			S			S	S	P	P				
90				CC	CC			O			S			S	S	P	P S	P S			
91				CC		Pr		O				S				P	P S	S			
92				CC		Pr		O								S	P S				
93				CC	CC	Pr		O						S		P					
94						Pr		O					S		P		S				
95								O				S			Pr S						
96								O					P S		S	Pr P	P S	P			
97								O					S	S	P		P	P Pr S			
98								O						S	S	P Pr	P Pr				
99								O					S	O	SPO	PO	P				
1900								O					Pr	POS	P	POS	P O				
01								O					Pr			POS					
02								O					Pr			P S					
03								O					Pr			P S					
04								P O					Pr			POS					
21	P														P S D r						

NUMBER OF REEDS   Pr = Proof

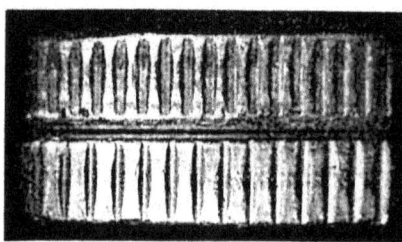

Morgan Dollar Edge Reeding Counts

1921 P I.R. & Normal

Use of 1878 S Reverse Working Dies For 1879 S

An **almost unique feature** of the 1878 S reverse working dies is the use of **two reverse dies** in both **1878** and **1879** to strike coins. These two dies of **1878 S** are **VAMs 1C/95** and **45/68** and both have **engraving** at the **wing-leg junction** to strengthen the over polished feather area. The 1878 S VAMs 1C and 95 with same reverse working die that struck coins were used again for the **1879 S VAMs 4/23/25** die combinations with three different obverse working dies to strike coins this following year. Similarly, the 1878 S VAMs 45/68 reverse working die struck coins in 1878 and again in **1879 S** with a different obverse die of **VAM 9.**

It should be noted that the **1878 Proof reverse die of C reverse design type** was used again in **1879** and **1880** to **strike proof coins.** But so far, no other reverse working dies have been identified that were used for more than one year to strike regular coins of the Morgan dollar series.

Available references–
1878 S Morgan Dollar Attribution Guide, by Leroy Van Allen & Craig Lickenbrock, Updated
　　March 2009.
A Guide To The 1879-S Reverse of 1878 Morgan Silver Dollars, by David Wang, 2001.

1878 S VAM 1C Wing Area

1878 S VAM 45 Engraved Wing Feather

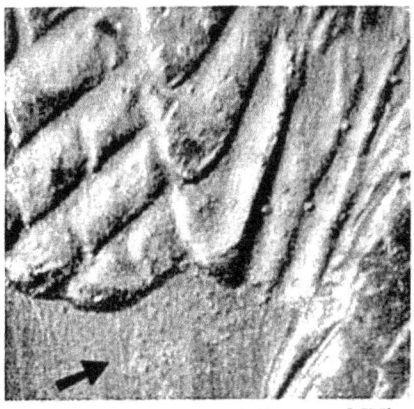

1879 S Rev 78 VAM 4 Engraved Wing
Feather, Rust Pitting

1879 S Rev 78 VAM 9 Engraved Wing Feather

Die Wear and Usage Flaws

Working dies were manufactured to be used to strike as many coins as possible to keep their preparation costs down. The stress on the die face of the constant impact on the planchet under **150 tons** of pressure eventually caused flaws in the working dies. These included fine line **die cracks** that could develop into **breaks** with **chunks** out of the die. Also, the constant friction of the planchet metal moving across the die face would abrade it's surface causing **wear lines**, **surface roughness** and **chips** to develop. In addition, **die rust pits** could develop on the die face and **clashed dies** could introduce unwanted extra images. Sometimes the working dies would be temporarily pulled from service and repairs were attempted by polishing the dies.

These die flaws are considered as errors as the dies normally wore out and weren't intentional die modifications. The press operator or supervisor would periodically inspect sample coins from each press in order to detect any usage and wear flaws. At some point in each die's life it would be judged no longer serviceable because of obvious flaws and be taken out of the coining press and retired. Minor **thin die cracks** usually developed fairly early on the large Morgan dollar dies and were not a reason to retire a die. Usually a **large visible break** or **chunk out of the die** needed to happen for die retirement. At other times a few dies were used beyond the normal wear state for retirement and a very rough and chipped die occurred on a few known dies.

Another usage flaw were **raised dots** on the coins from rust pitted dies that could have occurred before the die was put into service or even during an idle time when the die was installed in a coining press and the die face was not protected from rust. Another frequent die flaw that occurred during their usage were **clashed dies** when a planchet was accidently not fed between the obverse and reverse dies and they clashed together. This clashing would transfer part of the designs of one die to the opposing one. However, die clash marks are common and generally not listed as die varieties unless a **letter transfer** occurred during the clashing, which happened fairly often. This category also includes some **hub breaks** which appears on coins as **missing portions** of designs and occurred primarily in **1878.**

Hub Breaks

There are a number of instances where missing portions of a design occurred for a number of Morgan dollar working dies. This was the result of a defect forming on a **working hub** with part of the design **chipping off.** The defect shows up on the working dies as a raised defect which in turn is a **missing segment on the coin** when struck. Usually the working hubs were carefully inspected and taken care of so that defects in the working dies were minimized. However, the hasty preparation of the hubs and dies in 1878 because of the pressure to strike the required monthly quota of Morgan dollars resulted in defective working hubs and dies being used.

The most well known obverse hub defect is the **missing point of the fourth right star** on the **II type obverse.** The degree of broken fourth right star point varies as the metal flaked off the star point until most of it is missing on the hub. Also, the severity of the die polishing affected the amount of point remaining. There are so many working dies with the broken 4th right star that it has been designated a separate sub-variety type II 2. It appears with many different reverses of the **1878 P, S & CC** and many millions of coins were struck with this obverse defect.

Another **1878 P obverse hub break** is the progressive **break of the bottom serifs of N & M in UNUM.** This shows up on three working obverse dies of the II type and was the result of a deteriorating working hub before it was retired. Only several hundred coins with this hub break were struck by the three working dies.

The most well known reverse hub defect is the **broken r in Trust** on the **B² type reverse** to form Tiust in the extreme examples. This also was a progressive hub break and the severity was affected by the amount of die polishing. The hub break starts off as a chip off the top right serif of r and eventually deteriorates with it practically completely missing. This broken r hub defect appears on many working dies of the **1878 P, S and a few 1879 S Rev 78.** As a result, many millions of coins were struck with this reverse defect.

Another significant hub break on the **B² type reverse** is the **missing small upper portion of the o in God.** It appears on the working dies by itself or in combination with the broken r in Trust. Several million **1878 P** coins were struck with this open o in God hub defect.

A rarer reverse hub defect is the **broken bottom of the D in DOLLAR.** It is also a progressive die break that eventually shows as the bottom of the D almost completely missing. It shows up on several **1878 P** working dies of the **B² type reverse.**

A strange case is the **raised metal and die chips** in the **denticle spaces out into the field below 18** on the obverse. It occurs in various degrees on several of the **1879 P, O, S; 1880 S; 1881 O & S; and 1883 CC** working dies. It's severity can vary depending on the degree of die polishing. Since it appears on working dies over several years, this defect likely was on a working hub and possibly originated on a badly polished Master die.

It should be mentioned that a minor defect occurs on the **C³ type reverse.** It was on the master hub and die with incuse lines on the reverse legend letters.

Available references–
1878 P 7 Tail Feathers Morgan Dollar Attribution Guide, by Leroy Van Allen, revised November 2010.
Official Guide To The 1878 Reverse of '79 Varieties, by Mark Witkower, 2008.
A Guide to the Varieties of the 1878 Carson City Morgan Dollar, by John Roberts, 2010.
1878 S Morgan Dollar Attribution Guide, by Leroy Van Allen & Craig Lickenbrock, updated March 2009.
Official Guide to the Morgan Dollar Hit List 40, by Jeff Oxman, 2009.

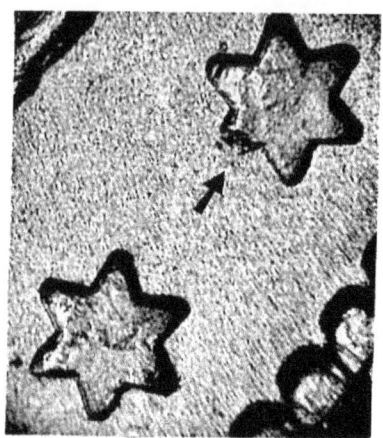

1878 P VAM 197 Broken 4th Right Star

1878 P VAM 141 Open O in God

1879 S VAM 3A Die Chips Below 18

1883 CC VAM 5 Chips Below 18

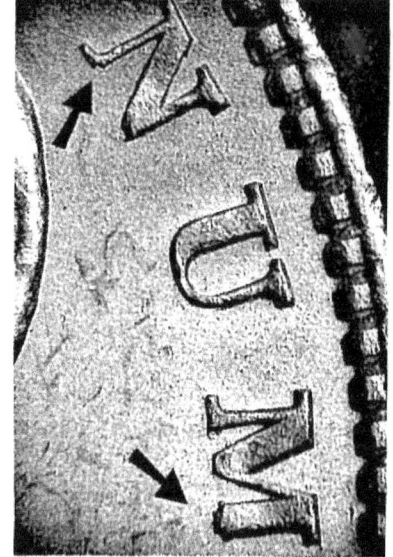

1878 P VAM 163 Broken r

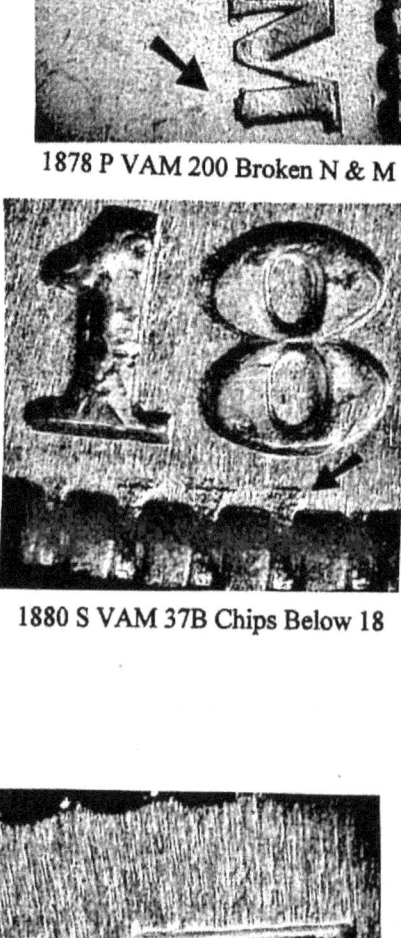

1878 P VAM 200 Broken N & M

1880 S VAM 37B Chips Below 18

1878 P VAM 195 Broken D Bottom

1879 P VAM 75 Chips Below 18

1881 O VAM 46 Chips Below 18

Lines in C³ Hub Letters

Lines in C³ Hub Letters

Die Breaks

As the working dies were used in the coining presses to strike coins, they developed die cracks, breaks and surface roughness in the fields at the periphery. This was the normal process and the dies were eventually removed from the coining presses and retired based on the judgement of the press operator or the supervisor. They typically examined a struck coin periodically to check if serious die flaws had developed. **Fine line shallow die cracks** weren't usually considered reasons to retire a die as they are extremely common. **Wide and high die breaks** that were fairly large and **heavy die wear** that began to make the fields rough and peripheral letters and stars weaker seem to be the point at which **most dies were retired**. Die breaks produced raised metal on coins whereas hub breaks produce missing metal on coins and are treated in a separate section on **Hub Breaks**.

For the listing of die varieties, die breaks have to be **wide and high readily visible to the naked eye**. Hundreds of the small die breaks have been listed out of the over 7,000 Morgan working dies produced. **Rim to rim die cracks** seem to develop into serious die weakness in that area with the die edge displaced and even rarely breaking away to form large raised metal call "cuds". Another serious die flaw that developed was a **radial die crack** that frequently split slightly apart and the two sides could became at different levels to form what is called a **displaced field die break**. Die chips are small breaks that could occur any place on the die. Tiny ones are very common as striking of coins abraded the die surface. Only when they become large enough to be **readily visible to the naked eye** are they listed.

The most visible and spectacular die break of the Morgan series is the **1888 O VAM 1B** so-called **Scarface** that was reported in 1979. Later die states have a die crack with chips and displaced field breaks that extend from the rim into the field to the Liberty head nose down across the cheek and into the upper neck. Early die states that only show a die crack into the field are much less in demand and bring much less premium. There is another **1888 O VAM 1A** with a prominent die crack and wide **break at R** in PLURIBUS on later die states with partial clashed letter 'E' below the eagle's tail feathers reported in 1976.

A number of the rare and spectacular **rim cud** large die breaks have been reported including the 1891 O VAM 9B and 15B, 1890 O VAM 4C, 1921 P VAM 19B and 1921 D VAMs 1N & 1X. Most were reported since 2000 except the 1921 P VAM 19B was reported in the mid 1980s. A large die chip above R in AMERICA of **1921 VAM 1B** called **Capped R** was reported in 1983. Probably the earliest really significant die break of the Morgan series is the **1887 P VAM 1A** so-call **Donkey Tail** with a large break at the bottom right of D in DOLLAR reported in 1964. Another early reported die break in 1974 is the **1889 P VAM 5A/19A** so-called **Bar Wing** with a break at the upper edge of the eagle's right wing below In that was caused by a die clash at that area. A spectacular die break on the **1881 S VAM 54A** reported in 1999 shows a **very long vertical die crack with wide breaks** on the eagle from the neck down thru the eagle's right leg to the rim below D in DOLLAR. A prominent die crack with **breaks thru 190** bottom is the **1900 O VAM 29A** reported in 1977. Some other significant die breaks are shown in the accompanying photographs.

Available references–

A Guide to the Varieties of the 1878 Carson City Morgan Dollar, by John Roberts, 2010.

1878 P 7 Tail Feather Morgan Dollar Attribution Guide, by Leroy Van Allen, Revised November 2010.

1878 S Morgan Dollar Attribution Guide, by Leroy Van Allen & Craig Lickenbrock, Updated March 2009.

Top 100 Morgan Dollar Varieties: The VAM Keys, by Michael Fey & Jeff Oxman, 4th ed., 2009.

Official Guide to the Morgan Dollar Hit List 40, by Jeff Oxman, 2009.

SSDC Official Guide to the Hot 50 Morgan Dollar Varieties, by Jeff Oxman, 2000.

Fun With 1921, by Rob Joyce, 2003.

1880 P VAM 45A Die Breaks Ear

1880 P VAM 45B Die Break 0

1882 P VAM 15A Die Break Ear

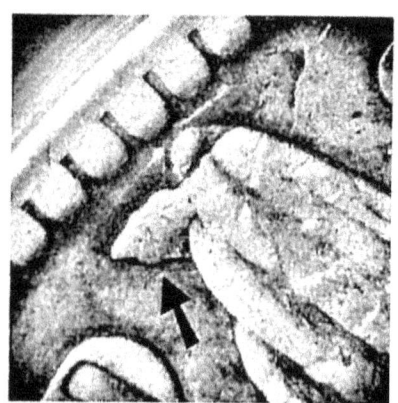

1883 O VAM 1C Die Break Wing Tip

1888 O VAM 1B Scar Face

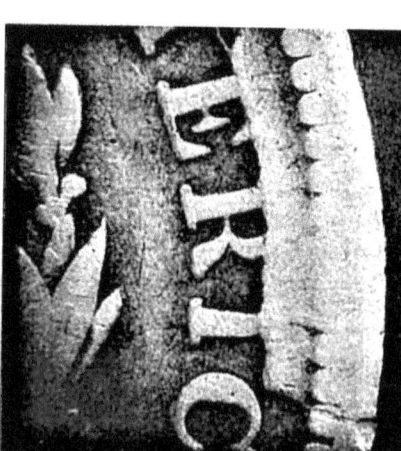

1890 O VAM 4C Break AMERIC

1890 S VAM 1I Breaks Left Wreath

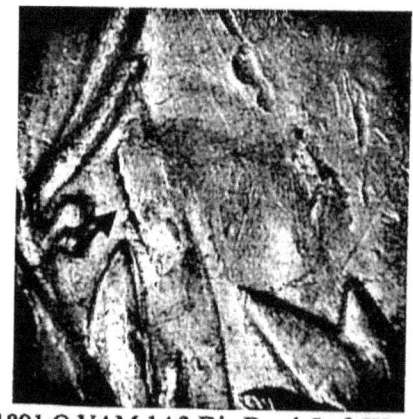

1891 O VAM 1A3 Die Break Left Wreath

1891 O VAM 15B Cud at ITE

1900 O VAM 19A Die Break Date

1900 O VAM 49A Die Breaks Wing Tip

1900 S VAM 12 A Die Break Star-U

1878 P VAM 113 Flake on Cheek

1878 S VAM 28 Die Chip

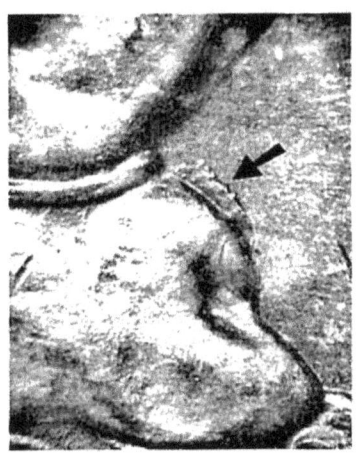

1880 S VAM 37A Die Break Cap Rear

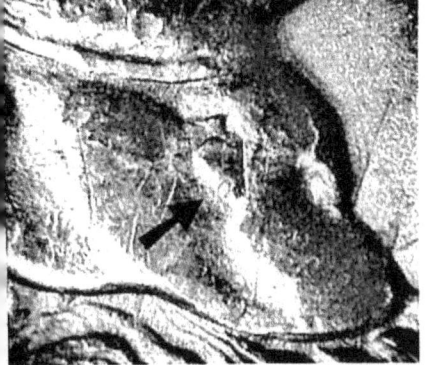

1880 P VAM 15A Die Break Lower Cap

1881 S VAM 54A Die Break Eagle

1887 P VAM 8B Die Break Above Cap

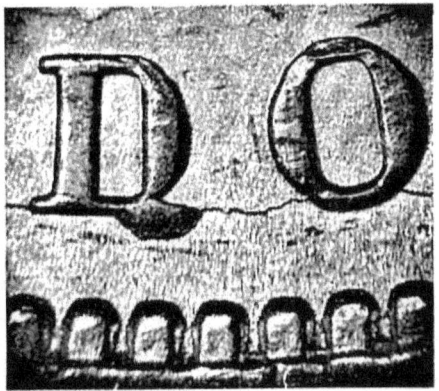

1887 P VAM 1A Donkey Tail Die Break D

1887 O VAM 5A Die Break Below 18

1888 O VAM 1A Die Break R (LDS)

1889 P VAM 19A Bar Wing Die Break

1891 O VAM 8A Die Break ME

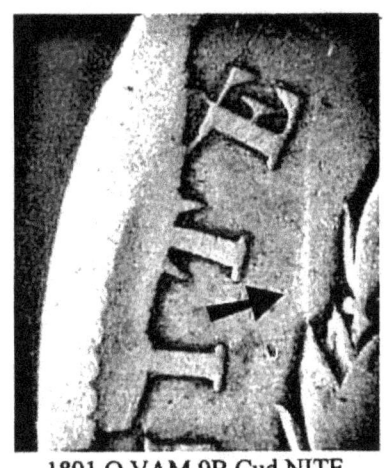

1891 O VAM 9B Cud NITE

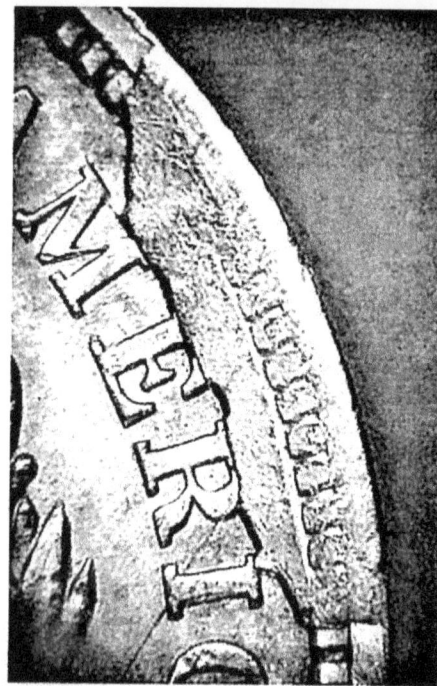

1921 P VAM 19B Rim Cud MERI

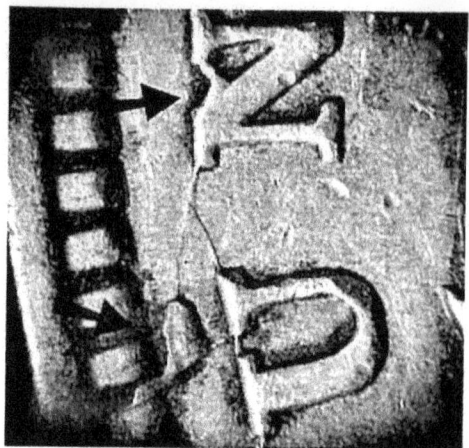

1921 P VAM 24A3 Die Breaks U & N

1921 D VAM 1B Capped R Die Break

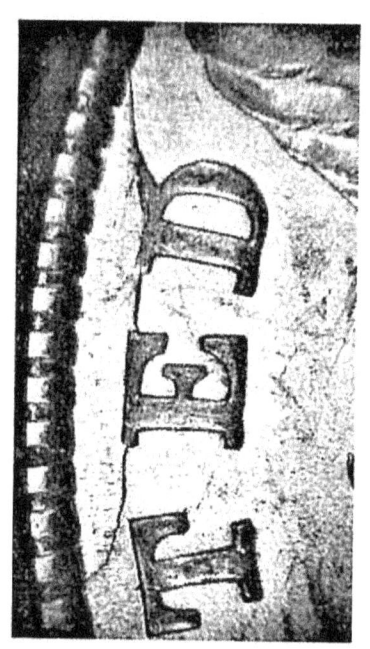

1921 D VAM 1N Die Break D (LDS)

1921 D VAM 1X Rim Cud at E-P

1921 D VAM 1J Retained Cud ED

Die Wear

Besides die cracks and breaks that occur during the normal die's lifetime, the surface was **abraded** from the **constant friction** of the planchet metal moving to fill the design cavities in the die. There was also **movement** of the **planchet metal outwards** due to the slight curvature of the die face from the basining. This outward metal flow formed the raised denticles and rim plus the edge reeding on the coin. The **periphery** of the die received the **most abrasion** during it's lifetime from the metal moving outward. Eventually the abrasion produces **radial die wear** lines as shown for the **1921 P VAM 72.**

Usually it was the die cracks and breaks that caused the dies to be retired from service. But sometimes the wear on the surface of the die became extreme which caused their retirement. Heavy die wear in the form of rough fields and die sinking around the peripheral letters and reverse wreaths is one example as shown for the **1888 P VAM 39A.** Another example is the formation of excessive die chips in the peripheral fields and around the letters and stars of **1890 O VAM 1F.** These examples are extreme die wear that normally the dies would have been retired before such wear happened. Usually the press operator or supervisor periodically examined some sample coins from the presses to determine the extent of the die flaws and wear and would make a judgement of when they started to become excessive and it was time to retire one of both dies.

Some unusual examples of extreme die wear include **strange die erosion** around 18 of **1887 P VAM 1K, heavy die wear** and **sinking** of the **1890 O VAM 13A,** and the **die chips** around the **stars** of **1889 P VAM 7A.**

There are also strange die wear patterns of **bands** above the wing tips of **1885 P VAM 1D** and **1886 P VAM 11.** Two unusual varieties show **trailing lines** from the reverse top **denticles** that is thought to be caused by die wear there from an **improperly basined die** or a **slightly tilted die.** This likely caused some planchet metal to flow **back towards the coin center** instead of normally outward. The **1921 S VAM 1Y** shows these trailing die wear lines from only one corner of the denticles whereas the **1921 S VAM 1L** shows the die wear lines from each corner of the denticles.

1885 P VAM 1D Banded Wing Tip

1887 P VAM 1K Erosion 18

1888 P VAM 39A Worn & Sunken Die

1888 O VAM 1G Crumbled Letters

1888 O VAM 31 Die Chips

1889 P VAM 51 Die Wear Ridges

1889 P VAM 7A Die Chips Stars

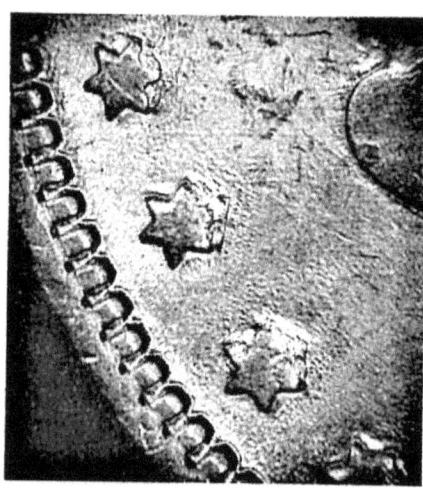

1889 O VAM 13B Crumbled Stars

1890 O VAM 13A Die Wear With Chips

1890 O VAM 1F Crumbled Field Below
Stars

1890 O VAM 29 Die Wear

1902 O VAM 4B Die Chips Stars

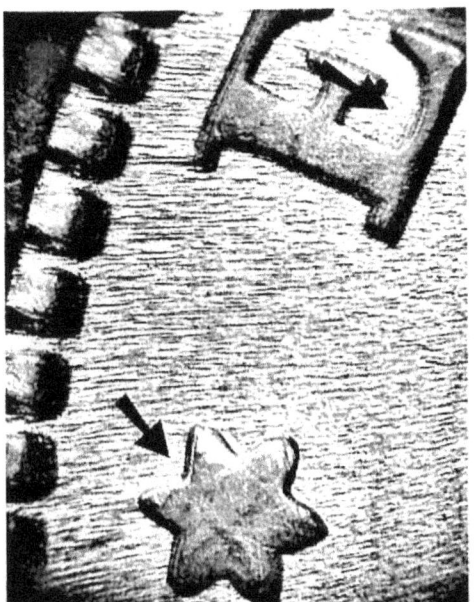

1921 P VAM 72 Typical Peripheral Radial
Die Wear Lines

1921 S VAM 1Y Trailing Die Wear Lines
Above STATES

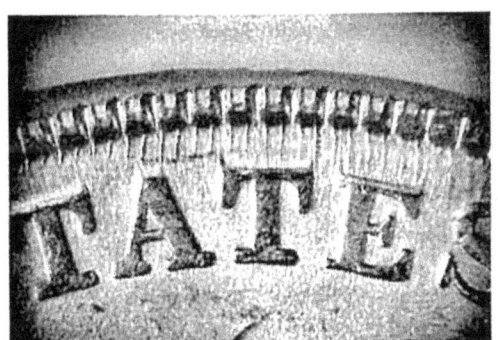

1921 S VAM 1L Trailing Die Wear Lines
Above STATES

Pitted Dies

Pitted dies are numerous **small raised dots** on coins scattered over small to large areas from rust on the die face. Only those <u>readily visible to the naked eye</u> are listed. Some 1883 P and O plus 1884 P have very fine raised dots on the Liberty head and/or eagle that aren't visible to the naked eye and aren't listed.

Morgan die faces were normally coated with grease when they were transported and stored to prevent the steel from rusting. However, some areas on the die faces may have accidently had this protective grease removed and exposed the steel to humid conditions to form rust. If the **rust dots** became deep enough, then the **tiny rust pits** in the die face resulted in **raised dots** on the struck coin. In addition, an unprotected die face in a coining press could also develop rust pits if left there for a sufficient number of days depending upon the humid conditions in a coining room.

Considering that over 7,000 pre-1921 Morgan dies were produced and somewhat less that actually struck the Morgan dollar series coin, the less than 50 listed dies with significant die rust pits is a very small percentage. In some cases, die rust pitting were polished out of the die if the pits weren't very deep. Other dies with extensive rust pitting may have been discarded and not used.

It is curious that most **rust dots** found on the coins were on the **reverse side**. Perhaps any noticeable rust its on the obverse die was cause for discarding them whereas the rust pits on the reverse die was not considered as objectionable. Also, the reverse die with a large wreath and feathers on the eagle tended to make the rust dots less noticeable compared to the open fields and Liberty head cheek and neck of the obverse die. One would think that the lower reverse die in the coining press would not be prone to more rusting than the upper obverse die . So it must have been the more noticeable and objectionable rust pitting on the obverse die that caused then to be discarded if it occurred.

Examples of rusted dies are shown in the accompanying photographs. Some of the earliest reported pitted reverse dies include the **1887 O VAM 1A/22A** with pitting at the olive branch and below the tail feathers, **1890 O VAM 4B/19** with pitting at NE, D and lower wreath, **1891 O VAM 1B** with pitting from the left of wreath down to the denticles, **1897 P VAM 1A/6A** with pitting from the tail feathers down to D in DOLLAR, **1921 P VAM 1A/41** with pitting in tail feathers, arrow feathers, reqth bow and ONE, **1921 P VAM 1E** with pitting at R in DOLLAR progressing to the lower tail feathers, LA, right star and eagle's beak, lower right wreath, AR in DOLLAR and A in AMERICA, **1921 S VAM 1C** with pitting around the arrow heads, wreath at right of bow and LA down to denticles and **1921 S VAM 1F** with pitting in the tail feathers down to wreath bow. Although rust pitting is most common on the lower reverse, there is an **1883 P VAM 1B** with coarse pitting all over the **Liberty head face**.

Available references–
Top 100 Morgan Dollar Varieties: The VAM Keys, by Michael Fey & Jeff Oxman, 4th ed., 2009.
SSDC Official Guide to the Hot 50 Morgan Dollar Varieties, by Jeff Oxman, 2000.
Official Guide to the Morgan Dollar Hit List 40, by Jeff Oxman, 2009.

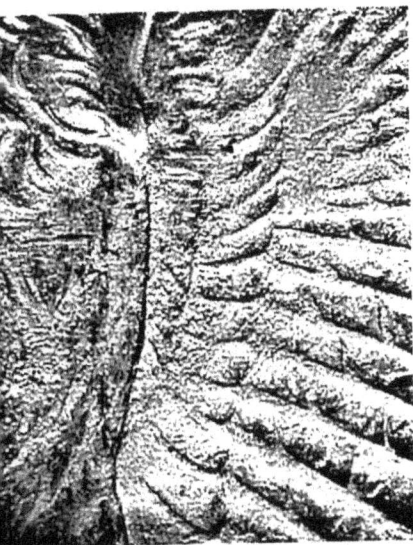

1878 S VAM 19A Rusted Die

1879 P VAM 37 Pitted Lower Reverse

1882 P VAM 1D Pitted Reverse

1885 P VAM 1B Pitted Reverse

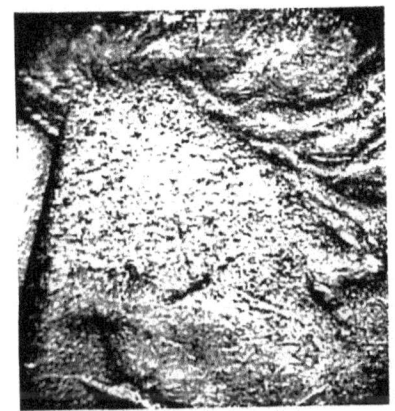

1883 P VAM 1B Die Rust Pits Forehead

1883 P VAM 1B Die Rust Pits Neck

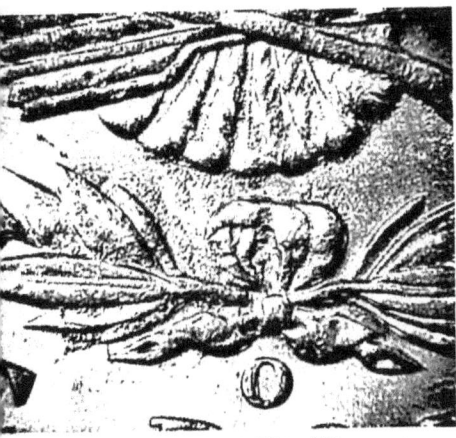

1887 O VAM 22A Pitted Reverse

1888 S VAM 1B Pitted Reverse

1890 O VAM 4B/19 Pitted Reverse

1891 O VAM 1B Pitted Reverse

1897 P VAM 6A Pitted Reverse

1904 O VAM 5A Pitted Reverse

1921 P VAM 1E Pitted Wreath Bow

1921 P VAM 3C Pitting UN

1921 P VAM 3C Pitting LL

1921 P VAM 3E Pitted Reverse Feathers

1921 P VAM 41 Pitted Reverse

1921 S VAM 1C Pitted Lower Right Revers

1921 S VAM 1E Pitted Reverse

Clashed Dies

Clashed dies have **parts** of the **opposite die design impressed into the die face**. It can occur if a blank planchet fails to be fed into the press coining chamber and the opposing dies come together. If the length of the hammer die stroke is long enough, it may impact the lower die with enough force to transfer some of the design parts of each die into the opposing die face. Because of the basining of the dies to produce a curvature on the die faces, the **closest space between the dies** are the fields around the **center outward** to about **half the distance to the rim**. These large central field areas are where die clash marks occur on the dies.

Die clash marks are fairly common on Morgan dollars and can occur at any point in the die's lifetime. The obverse die can show clash marks as a **raised diagonal line** from the **Liberty head neck**, **raised lines** at the **lips** and **back of the Phrygian cap** near the ribbon end. The reverse die can show a **vertical raised line** at the **top of the eagle's right wing, marks** at the left side of the **eagle's neck,** Liberty head **profile** at right side of the **left wreath** and **sideways vee** at the top inside of the **right wreath**. However, the common nature of these clash marks makes them generally not collectible. Only when **clashed letters** are transferred do clashed die varieties become collectible.

The raised full clashed **'E'** below the eagle's left tail feathers is from the obverse E in LIBERTY and has been known since 1963 for the **1886 O VAM 1A, 1889 O VAM 1A and 1891 O VAM 1A**. They bring substantial premiums, especially for the rarer 1889 O. Partial clashed 'E' letters below the eagle's tail feathers were reported in the 1970s for eight different dates of 1878 P, 1880 P, 1883 O, 1884 P, 1887 P, 1888 O, 1889 O and 1891 O. It wasn't until **1997** that a very bold **incuse In** from the reverse was reported next to the **Liberty head neck** on the **1889 P VAM 23A**. That discovery ushered in a **new era in collecting clashed die letters** besides the 'E' below the tail feathers. Clashed letters from In, G of the reverse motto have since been reported at the neck.

There are hundreds of clashed dies now known and listed with clashed letters with most reported since 2003. Some are faint and only small partial letters show that are interesting but hardly bring any premium prices. Also, as dies wore out or were polished to remove the die clash marks, the clashed letters can fade out or disappear. Some clashed letter locations are prominent and easily seen such as letters at the Liberty head neck or below the eagle's tail feathers. Other locations are fairly well hidden such as in the lower hair curls and require a good magnifying glass to see.

The accompanying photographs show some of the more prominent clashed letters on working dies. Besides the very visible full 'E' below the tail feathers of 1886 O, 1889 O and 1891 O, some of the partial 'E' varieties are fairly visible. The most prominent and first reported obverse clashed letter remains the **1889 P VAM 23A** with a very deep incuse **In** at the Liberty head neck and **st,** from Trust on the reverse, in the lower right Liberty head hair vee. The **1878 P VAM 41C 7/8** Tail Feather also has a pretty strong clashed **In**. The **1880 P VAM 32A** has one of the strongest clashed **M** above d in God from the obverse designer's initial and in 2003 was the first reported clashed M. The **1883 O VAM 22A** shows a clashed **D** for DOLLAR and **O** from the O mint mark at the obverse wheat leaves and was the first reported clashed legend letter D on the obverse in 2003. The **1883 O VAM 36** shows the **DO** clashed letters at the wheat leaves. The clashed **t** at the lower right hair vee of **1887 P VAM 3** is very strong and the first reported clashed letter at that location in 2003. The **1888 O VAM 1A** with clashed **O** mint mark at the right wheat leaf was the first O mint mark clash also reported in 2003. The **1901 O VAM 1A** has an exceptionally strong clashed **t** at the lower right hair vee. The **1902 O VAM 26A** shows a very strong double clashed **G** at the Liberty head neck.

An **unusual** case of clashed die rotation is the **1887 O VAM 30A** that shows bars under the tail feathers of the letters **TY** from the obverse LIBERTY. The **1891 O VAM 14A** has the **unusual** clashed **God We below** the obverse hair line and the clashed **M** initial from the obverse shows **below** the d of God. A **large shift** of multiple clash marks is shown for the **1886 P VAM 1C** with two widely separated **clash vees** with 3 clashes each due to die rotation.

The **king** of clashed die varieties is the scarce **1889 O VAM 1A LDS** with **9 identified clashed letters** including a **double clashed 'E'**. There is clashed **BER** below the tail feathers, clashed **M** above W in We, clashed **G** at the Liberty head neck, clashed **t** at the lower right hair vee, clashed **D** from DOLLAR at the wheat kernels, clashed **O** mint mark at the right wheat leaf and clashed **"R"** tick from AMERICA at the Phrygian cap back edge.

Available references–

Elite Clashed Morgan Dollars, by Mark Kimpton, Sheriden Books, 2005.
A Guide to the Varieties of the 1878 Carson City Morgan Dollar, by John Roberts, 2010.
1878 P 7 Tail Feathers Morgan Dollar Attribution Guide, by Leroy Van Allen, Revised November 2010.
1878 S Morgan Dollar Attribution Guide, by Leroy Van Allen & Craig Lickenbrock, Updated March 2009.
1902 O Morgan Dollar Series Attribution Guide, by Alan Scott, 2010.
1904 O Morgan Dollar Series Attribution Guide, by Alan Scott, 2010.
Top 100 Morgan Dollar Varieties: The VAM Keys, by Michael Fey & Jeff Oxman, 4th ed., 2009.
SSDC Official Guide to the Hot 50 Morgan Dollar Varieties, by Jeff Oxman, 2000.
Official Guide to the Morgan Dollar Hit List 40, by Jeff Oxman, 2009.
Lady Liberty Letters, by Leroy Van Allen, *Numismatist,* February 2004.

Die Clash Marks Cap Back

Die Clash Marks Top Right Wreath

86 O VAM 1A Single Clashed BER

1891 O VAM 1A Clashed BERT

1891 O VAM 1A Clashed D & O Mint Mark

89 O VAM 1A Doubled Clashed BER

1889 O VAM 1A Clashed D & O Mint Mark

1889 O VAM 1A Clashed G

1889 O VAM 1A Clashed t

1889 O VAM 1A Clashed M

1880 P VAM 25B Clashed In

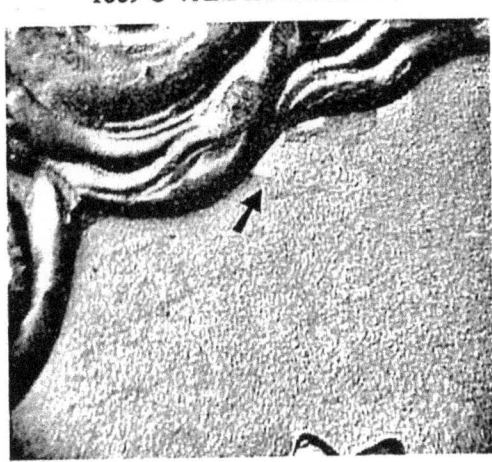

1902 O VAM 45A Clashed st

1902 O VAM 45A Strongly Clashed Wreath

1878 P VAM 84A Clashed Partial E

1880 P VAM 39A Clashed Partial E

1883 O VAM 22A Clashed Partial E

1884 P VAM 2A Clashed Partial E

1887 P VAM 1B Clashed Partial E

1888 O VAM 1A Clashed Partial BER

1889 O VAM 20A Clashed Partial E

1891 O VAM 3A Clashed Partial ER

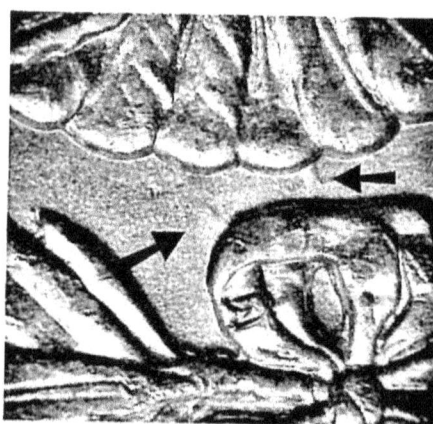

1887 O VAM 30A Clashed Partial TY

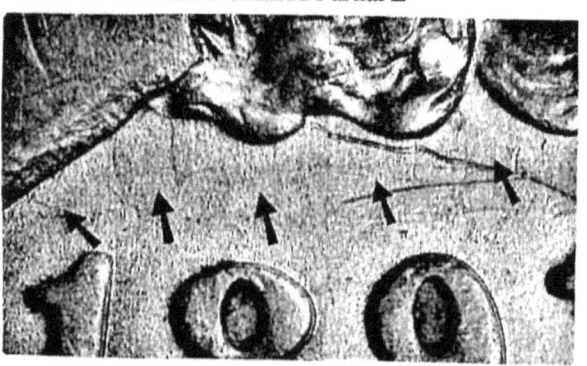

1891 O VAM 14A Clashed Partial God We

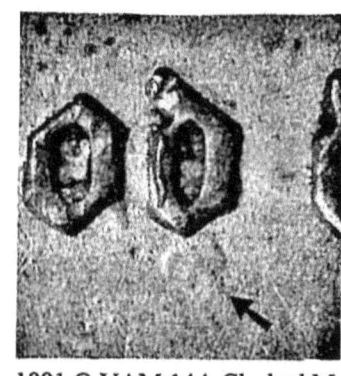

1891 O VAM 14A Clashed M

1886 P VAM 1C 3 + 3 Clashed Vees

1889 P VAM 23A Strongly Clashed In

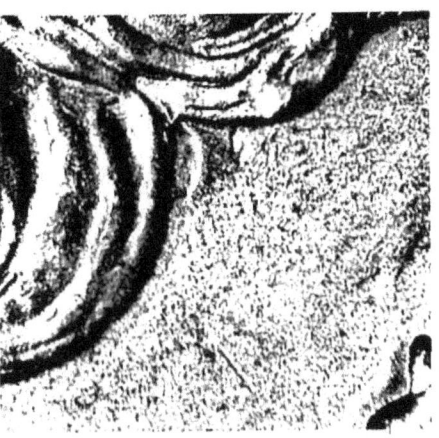

1889 P VAM 23A Strongly Clashed st

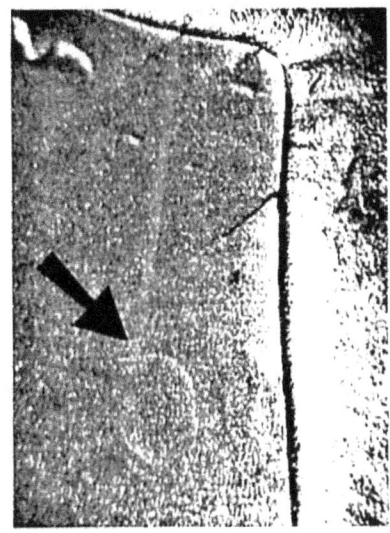

1878 P VAM 41A Clashed n & G

1880 P VAM 32A Strongly Clashed M

1883 O VAM 22A Clashed D & O Mint Mark

1883 O VAM 36A Clashed D & O Mint Mark

1887 P VAM 3A Clashed t

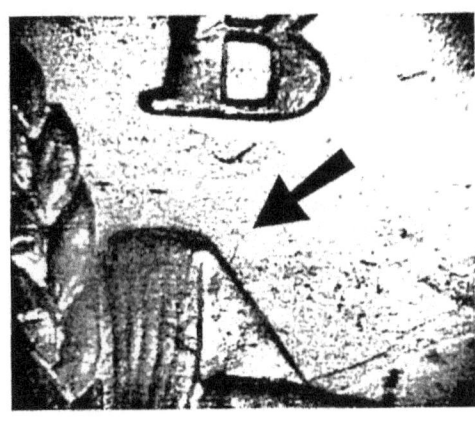

1888 O VAM 1A Clashed O

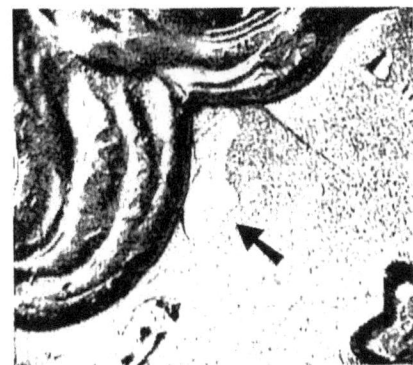

1901 O VAM 1A LDS Strongly Clashed t

1902 O VAM 26A Double Clashed G

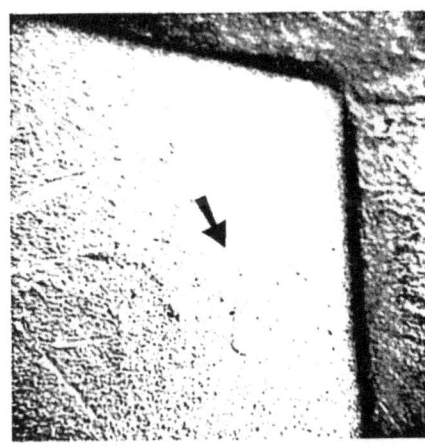

1878 P VAM 2A Clashed In

1878 P VAM 42A Clashed In

1880 P VAM 32A Clashed In

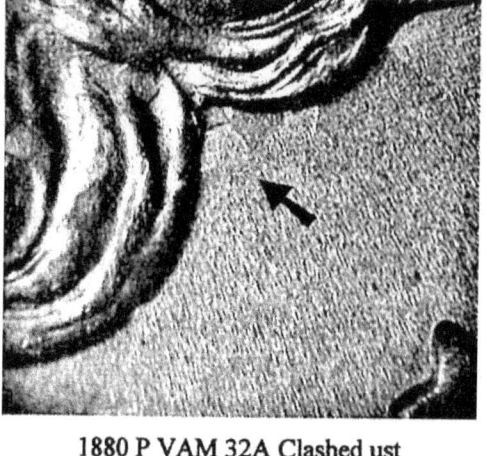

1880 P VAM 32A Clashed ust

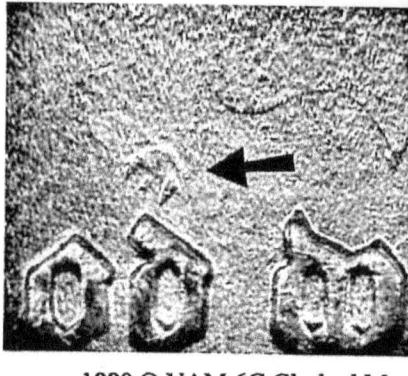

1880 O VAM 6C Clashed M

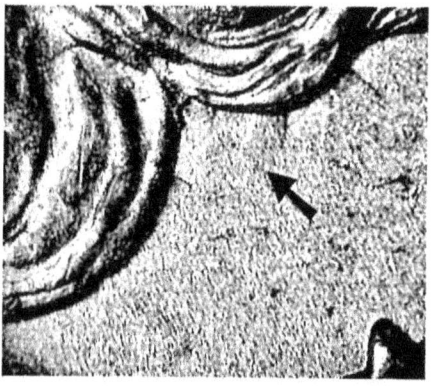

1880 O VAM 6C Clashed ust

1882 O VAM 29A Clashed G

1885 P VAM 9A Clashed n

1890 O VAM 1B Clashed In

1890 O VAM 4A Clashed G

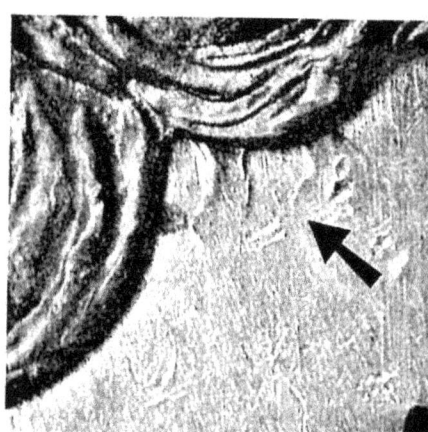

1898 S VAM 15A Clashed st

1901 O VAM 39A Clashed I

1901 O VAM 25A Clashed st

1921 S VAM 28A Clashed In With Lines

COUNTERFEITS

Counterfeit Morgan dollars have been around for over a century. Before the Morgan dollar disappeared from general circulation in the early 1960s because of the rising price of silver, most counterfeits were made for circulation. The price of silver was around 60 cents or less per ounce from 1893 thru 1917 and again from 1921 thru 1945. A Morgan dollar contains 0.77 ounce of silver and counterfeiters could use about 50 cents worth of silver, combined with a little copper, to produce a counterfeit dollar with the correct silver fineness and weight. These could be passed into circulation for one dollar since there were few collectors of Morgan dollars that could detect them and most genuine Morgan dollar dates were readily available from local banks at face value.

Common date counterfeit Morgan dollar coins were made for **general circulation** usually when the price of silver was **well below** the **$1.29 per ounce** that matched the one dollar face value for the 0.77 ounce of silver in a Morgan dollar. **Scarce** Morgan dollar dates that fetched **premium prices** were later counterfeited for sale to coin collectors and dealers. Only a few dates had significant premiums that were targets for counterfeiters before collecting Morgan dollars became popular with rising prices beginning in the mid-1960s. Since then, the counterfeiting of the greater number of expensive dates has become more **prevalent** and common dates much less so. Expensive **key date** Morgan dollars should now be **authenticated** by reliable grading services.

There are **three** general methods for the fabrication counterfeit coins. One of the popular counterfeiting methods of years ago was to make a **cast copy** of a coin. It was relatively simple and did not require much equipment or skill. Another method was to **alter a common date** to become a more valuable date by adding or removing a mint mark or altering a date digit. The third method was to prepare **counterfeit dies** and then use similar equipment of the U.S. Mints to prepare planchets and to strike counterfeit coins. The following sections briefly discuss each of these counterfeiting methods with some example photographs.

Cast Copies

Before the Morgan dollars disappeared from general circulation in the early 1960s because of the rising price of silver, most counterfeits were made for **circulation**. Many of these counterfeits were **cast coins** and most were **crudely made** of base (lead) metal using **sand molds**. They had **many defects** including rough appearance with extra lumps of metal, weak detail and under weight. They were typically passed as circulated pieces to unsuspecting general public. But more knowledgeable collectors and dealers of the 1960s and later culled most of these crudely made cast counterfeits from circulation and the later circulated coin inventories and collections. They can usually be easily identified by the raised casting lumps, roughness in the fields, dull coin ring, underweight, diffuse design detail and leaving marks on paper for those that are lead based.

The accompanying photographs show a crudely cast **1885 CC** with **muled 1921 D type reverse**, very underweight and crudely engraved CC mint mark. Another obvious cast counterfeit is the **1921 P** with **hand engraved date digits**, casting roughness and underweight.

Later more modern casting materials and techniques can yield much better cast counterfeits with the correct weight, diameter, coin ring and metal composition. Still, the isolated casting defect or flaw, rounded or diffuse design edges, incorrect edge reeding and lack of slid lines in the reeding of a die struck coin usually makes these later cast counterfeits identifiable with a strong hand magnifying glass or 10X- 30X stereo microscope. However, even the best counterfeit can be positively identified by x-ray diffractometry or metallographic microscope examination because the crystalline structure of cast coins is different than the disturbed metal flow of a die struck coin.

Coin Alteration

The most **common** form of **coin alteration** is to **grind or cut away a mint mark** using jeweler's tools. Some known examples are 1894 O changed to 1894 P, 1901 O to 1901 P and the infamous change of 1895 O to a 1895 P counterfeit (Mostly to fill a collectors desire to have something representing the scarce expensive date.). Always examine the mint mark area below the reverse wreath bow for telltale polishing or tool marks on expensive scarce P mint coins or incorrect die variety for the date.

Mint marks can be added to lower priced P mint coins or mint mark coins that have had the mint mark removed. Genuine mint marks can be removed from branch mint coins and glued or soldered onto the counterfeit coin. Always check the mint mark of an expensive branch mint coin to make sure it is the proper design type and that there are sharp edges where the mint mark merges into the flat field. There should be no gaps there characteristic of an added mint mark. Mint marks have been added to P mint coins to fabricate counterfeit 1889 CC, 1892 S, 1895 S, 1896 S, 1903 S and 1904 S. Sometimes these added mint mark coins will show die variety features of other dates which is an immediate tip off of an altered coin and an advantage that die variety collectors have in counterfeit detection.

A more recent counterfeit threat of coin alteration is the embossed mint mark. A hole is drilled from the coin edge to under the mint mark area. A tool with the mint mark shape at the end is forced upwards at the mint marks area to raise the mint mark shape. The edge hole is then plugged and polished over. Usually the embossed mint mark can be detected by the lack of sharp edges at the top or where it meets the field, incorrect shape, or flaws at the edge reeding below the mint mark area.

Date alteration is much less of a threat because of their large size. For example, an 1898 S was altered to an 1893 S by reshaping the 8 into a 3 digit. But the shape of the 3 wasn't quite correct for the 1893 and the known die markers for a genuine 1893 S weren't present. Dates can also be altered by grinding down one or both last digits and gluing or soldering new digits there. But the large size of the digit makes their transplant very difficult without telltale gaps and flaws.

Counterfeit Die Struck Coins

Counterfeit coins struck from counterfeit dies can duplicate the U.S. Mint's coin production process and are thus possibly a more accurate copy of genuine coins. They also allow the counterfeiter to mass produce counterfeit coins rather than slow time consuming casting or altering individual coins. Die struck coins, on the other hand, requires sophisticated equipment for planchet production, making of steel dies and collars and the use of large coining presses.

There are numerous ways to produce the counterfeit steel dies. Hand cut engraved dies usually show numerous design flaws easily recognized. Tracing the design of a genuine coin and simultaneously engraving the design on the face of a steel bar allows more accurate design reproduction but there is a loss of some design detail and often spiral engraving lines will show on the die. Other design transfer techniques, such as fusing powered metal that loses some size dimensions, impacting a genuine coin at high speed on a die face, spark erosion which leaves tiny pits or electromechanical machining that loses design detail have flaws usually detectable.

Perhaps the greatest counterfeiting threat are die struck coins made form cast counterfeit dies. This technique has evolved over the last century from using relatively crude sand cast molds to sophisticated multiple transfer methods of wax, plaster and/or molten metal transfer steps to a final metal-to-metal design transfer to produce the final die. Some of these design transfer steps can add imperfections and careful inspection of the counterfeit coins can reveal the same imperfections on multiple coins. Sometimes there is an incorrect mating of the obverse design with the reverse design that can be an immediate tip-off. All of these two to three steps in design transfer can result in lessened sharp detail where the design meets the field with excessive rounding, loss of fine polishing lines of a genuine copied coin or raised dots and flaws. The edge reeding count can be incorrect but can have collar slid lines indicating the coin was die struck in a collar. Also, incorrect die variety signs of date or design doubling from another year or even incorrect design type for the year can help identify these die struck counterfeit coins

A recent unusual counterfeit 1889 CC was in a fake PCGS holder with the correct I.D. number. As shown in the accompanying photographs, there was sharp detail on both the obverse and reverse with some luster present. It's look was somewhat strange however, with extremely few bag marks in the fields. The weight and diameter were correct and the reeding had slid lines indicating it was die struck. The reeding count of 180 was incorrect which should have been 177 or 178. There were numerous raised dots in the obverse fields and the reverse had the same doubled CC mint mark as the 1884 CC VAM 5 of an incorrect prior year.

One of the most **notorious and earliest counterfeiting** operations using **cast counterfeit dies** to struck many counterfeit Morgan dollars was the so-called **Micro O mint mark series.** Genuine very tiny O mint marks exist in circulated and uncirculated condition for some of the 1880 O and 1899 O coins. In his 1963 booklet, *Die Varieties of Morgan Silver Dollars,* Francis X. Klaes had photographs of Micro O varieties for 1880, 1896, 1899, 1900, and 1902. Some numismatists had been suspect even in 1963 that the 1896, 1900 and 1902 Micro O coins were early 20th century copies. But this was not widely known and collectors eagerly sought these three Micro O dates of 1896, 1900 and 1902 that were only rarely found in circulated condition. They had the correct weight, diameter and silver content but similar defects. In 2000, Numismatic Guaranty Corporation stopped certifying them. Finally, in 2005 it was documented and proven that these three Micro O dates were cast die struck counterfeits and the grading services stopped authenticating them, except a few services do still grade with a counterfeit notation. A 1900 O Micro O was listed as very good condition in the B. Max Mehl June 17, 1947 catalog of the Will W. Neil Collection, proving that this counterfeit had been in circulation for many decades and likely was counterfeited around 1902 when the 1896 O, 1900 O and 1902 O coins were available for copying.

But the story of these Micro O gets even more **interesting** after the 2005 expose. A much rarer **1901 Micro O counterfeit** was reported in 2007. From 2005 thru 2011, collectors reported **additional** cast die counterfeit circulated coins of the 1896 O, 1900 O, 1901 O and 1902 O dates that were **related** to the same four Micro O counterfeit dates thru the use of the same obverse or reverse counterfeit dies. Currently, the known Micro O and related counterfeit dies and collars includes **8 obverse dies, 11 reverse dies and 6 collars** for a total of **20 die combinations** that all have similar circulated appearances and casting defects. Each coin had slid marks on the edge reeding confirming that they were die struck and multiple circulated examples have been found for most die combinations. With each counterfeit die possibly striking an average of 1,000 coins, perhaps 10,000 counterfeit or more coins may have been struck and released into general circulation early in the 20th century. Amazingly, they were all likely produced around 1902 when uncirculated coin specimens were available in the New Orleans Mint area to copy and the price of silver was 60 cents per ounce. Only about 50 cents worth of silver plus a little copper enabled the counterfeiters to pass these counterfeits Morgan dollars into general circulation for one dollar of goods or services, or deposit them in banks. There may still be more new die combinations yet to be found that are related to these counterfeit dies of these four dates that are part of the so-called Micro O counterfeiting operation.

The accompanying photographs show the **tilted Micro O mint mark** copied from a **1899 O genuine Micro O coin** and copied on the counterfeit coins. Some identifiers are also as shown for these related counterfeits including **incorrect reverse types, die gouge lines at UM in UNUM** for 1900 O or **filled 9 and 0 digits** on the 1901 O coins.

Available references–
Micro O and Other Counterfeit Morgan and Peace Dollars, by Leroy Van Allen, revised February 2011.
Morgan Dollar "Micro O" Fakes, by Leroy Van Allen, *Numismatist,* July 2011.
Die Varieties Of Morgan Silver Dollars, by Francis X. Klaes, 1963.
Top 100 Morgan Dollar Varieties: The VAM Keys, by Michael Fey & Jeff Oxman, 4th ed., 2009.
Comprehensive Catalog and Encyclopedia of Morgan & Peace Dollars, by Leroy C. Van Allen and A. George Mallis, WorldWide Ventures, 4th ed., 1998, Chapter 15, Detecting Counterfeits.

The Comprehensive U.S. Silver Dollar Encyclopedia, by John W. Highfill, Highfill Press, 1992, Chapters 19 & 20.

Morgan and Peace Dollar Textbook, by Wayne M. Miller, Adam Smith Publishing, 1982, Chapter VIII.

Numismatic Forgery, by Charles M. Larson, 2004.

Counterfeit, Mis-Struck and Unofficial U.S. Coins, by Don Taxay, Arco Publishing, 1963.

1885 CC Small Engraved CC

1885 CC D Reverse

1921 P Hand Engraved Date

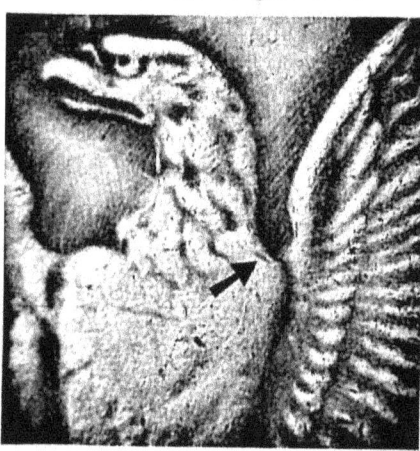

1889 O Counterfeit D Wing-Neck Gap

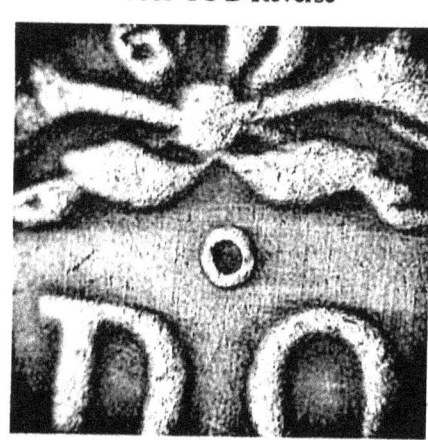

1889 O Counterfeit Fake O Mint Mark

1896 S Added Mint Mark to 1896 P

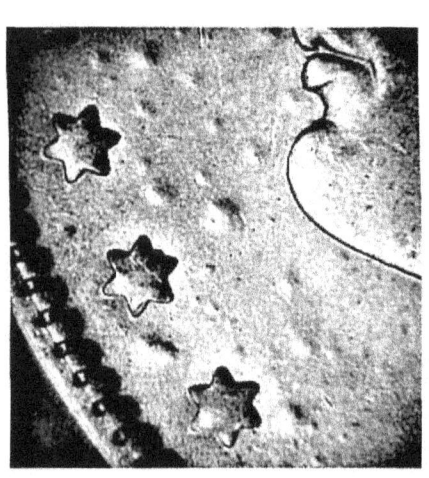

1889 CC Counterfeit Round Raised Dots

1889 CC Counterfeit CC/CC
of 1884 CC VAM 5

1903 S Tracing Lines Left Field

1899 O Variety 6, Micro O Tilted Far Right

1901 O Genuine Medium O Tilted Right

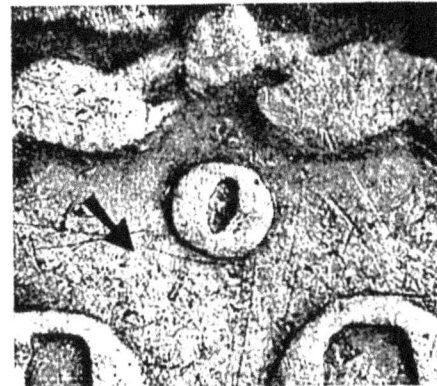

1901 O Counterfeit Micro O Tilted Far Right, Indent

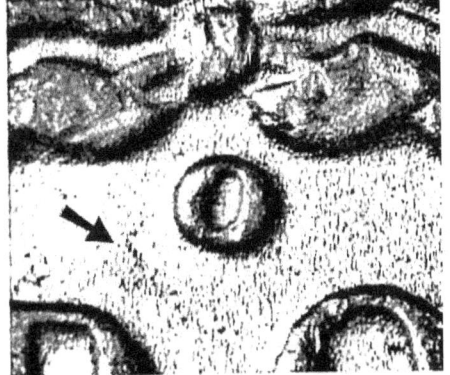

1896 O Counterfeit Micro O Tilted Far Right, Indent

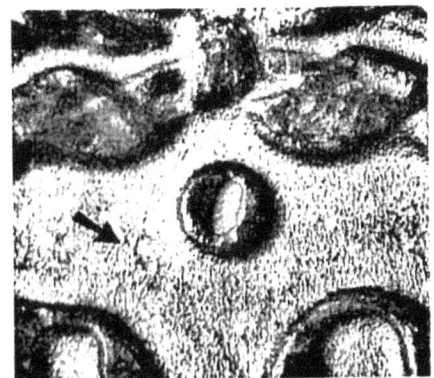

1900 O Counterfeit Micro O Tilted Far Right, Indent

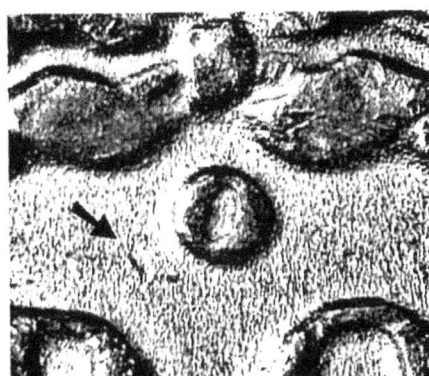

1902 O Counterfeit Micro O Tilted Far Right, Indent

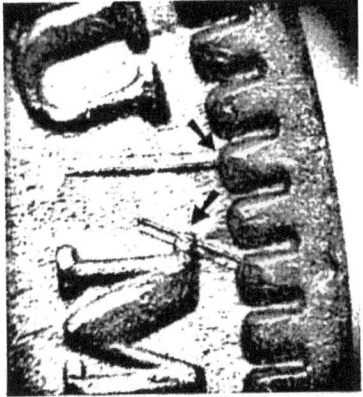

1900 O Counterfeit Micro O, Lines Between UM

1896 O Counterfeit Medium O, Wide Wing-Neck Gap

1902 O Counterfeit Micro O, Narrow Wing-Neck Gap

1902 O Counterfeit Rounded Wing Edge

1896 O Counterfeit Dots LLAR

1900 O Counterfeit Dots LLAR

1901 O Counterfeit Medium O, Partially Filled 90

PLANCHET ERRORS

Errors on the planchets occur during their fabrication and generally each error on a resulting coin is unique. The metal content of 90% silver and 10% copper was strictly controlled to produce the metal bars and punched planchet discs of 0.900 fineness of silver required by law. Sampling of coins produced by each mint were sent to the **Director of the Mint** and the **Annual Assay Commission** where they were **tested** each year to assure the coins were of the proper fineness. That leaves accidental errors on the planchets, split planchets and even raised bubbles of occluded gas. Inspection and counting of the coins by hand before 1904 culled out the most obvious planchet errors, so they are fairly rare for the earlier Morgan dollars, but more frequent for the 1921.

Impure Metal and Laminations

These two types of planchet errors are related and are from **impurities in bullion melt**. When the silver strips are rolled down to the planchet thickness, these impurities may be visible on the surface as discolored **dark streaks** from the rolling operation. The impurities can be of various thickness and sometimes a thin layer of silver is separated over the impurities as a **lamination**. Some accompanying photographs show typical impure metal streaks and laminations. Small areas of impure metal or laminations may lower the value of a coin, but very large areas may be of higher value to collectors.

Clipped Planchets

Missing portions of the edge of a planchet and resulting coin are called **clips**. They may have the shape of **curves**, **straight** or **ragged**. Over lapping punches on the silver strip created curved clips, punches at the end of a strip resulted in straight clips and punches on a broken area created ragged clips. The automatic weighing of planchets, hand feeding of planchets into the coining presses and the hand inspection and counting of Morgan dollar coins resulted in the elimination of the obvious large clips. A few small rim clips are known however, as shown in the accompanying photographs.

Split Planchets

Impurities or **weak metal layers** completely thru the planchets may have resulted in a separation in the coin, usually in a radial direction. The stress in the metal from the striking of a coin can also separate a weak boundary layer. Few split planchet errors are known for the Morgan dollars of 1904 and prior years because of the **ring test** performed at the final coin inspections that was used to detect defective planchets.

Occluded Gas

Gas trapped when the silver ingot was cast could have remained when the strips were rolled out. If the trapped gas was near the planchet surface, then it may result in **raised bubbles** on the struck coin. However, occluded raised bubbles are **very rare** on Morgan dollars. Raised bubbles can also be seen on coins that have been heated or been in a fire, but that is usually obvious with dark areas or deformed areas on the coin.

Planchet Striations

The final step in preparing the silver strips before punching out the round planchet discs was passing the strips thru the **draw bench**. This produced the uniform final thickness of the silver strips. Starting in 1901, the new Philadelphia Mint eliminated use of draw benches since the new rolls could achieve the required uniform strip thickness. Other mints continued to use draw benches thru the end of Morgan dollar production in 1904. If the strips **weren't properly coated with tallow** or the **draw bench jaw edges became ragged**, then **grooves** could appear on the **surface of the silver strips**. These **incuse lines** could show up on the raised areas on the coin where the metal was not forced against the **die cavities** as much as in the fields, typically on the **Liberty head cheek and neck** and the **eagle's breast and legs**.

Impure Metal Streak

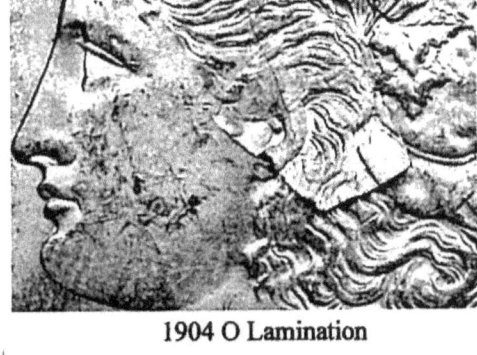

1904 O Lamination

1921 P Rim Clip

1921 S Split Planchet

1921 P Ragged Edge Clip

1921 P Impure Metal Streak & Lamination

1888 S Occluded Gas

Planchet Striations

STRIKING ERRORS

There are a large number of different types of striking of coin errors that occurred on Morgan dollar coins. Most are **fairly rare** for the Morgan dollars because of the **large coin size** and the **individual coin inspections** at each mint. Large obvious striking errors have mostly been found and reside in collections. Lesser spectacular striking errors can still be found.

Unique striking error coins can occur when individual planchets aren't positioned correctly between the coin dies or in the collar. This resulted in **off-center, broadstruck and partial collar** errors. **Misaligned dies** in the coining presses resulted in **slightly narrow or wide rims** on either the obverse or reverse of the coin and many coins could have been struck with this error. **Weakly struck** coins with weak or missing coin detail could have happened on a number of similar coins but usually the press operator soon corrected the striking pressure. **Struck thru** coins could be unique or lasted only a few struck coins until the foreign grease or scrap metal wore down or fell away. They are only somewhat scarce. **Multiple struck** coins are <u>very rare</u>. **Machine doubling** where the dies moved during the striking of the coin is **very common**, especially on the reverse of the Morgan dollar. **Rotated dies** where the obverse and reverse dies aren't in the normal upside down relationship are fairly scare but can result in **multiple coins** of the same or varying degrees of rotation for a given date. Some photographs are shown of the various types of striking errors.

Press Adjustment Errors

When dies were first installed in the coining presses, the die striking throw distance and die striking pressure had to be adjusted to bring up all of the coin detail. Some **die adjustment coins** with weak detail resulted during the initial die set-up, but these were normally melted as defective coins. A few were inadvertently released into circulation but are **very rare for Morgan dollars** with appreciable missing coin detail. **Out of level dies** could produce weakly struck coins on one side, but again are rare. If the dies were not aligned exactly on center vertically, then a **misaligned die** could occur with one coin side showing thin and wide rims opposite each other. They are rarely found but can produce multiple coins if the misalignment wasn't soon corrected. **Slightly low striking pressure** that resulted in weak peripheral lettering and stars or center hair detail and is fairly common and doesn't affect the coin value, unless very noticeable.

Weak Strikes

Each Morgan die was basined to give a slight curvature to the die face. This allowed the proper metal flow from coin center out to the rim and edge reeding to make the design brought up evenly across the coin. Each mint basined their dies because the different coining presses at the various mints required slight differences in the basining process. Nevertheless, while the **P** and **CC** mint coins were **usually evenly struck**, the S mint coins typically had **fully struck coin centers** and weaker peripheries, while the **O** mint coins typically had **weak centers of hair over the ear** and eagle's breast feathers with fully struck rims. Usually these design relief variations on the coins don't affect their value unless there is extreme flatness to the ear and hair over the ear. On some coins of mostly O mints, there can be weak eagle's breast feathers detail with a little depression in the middle of the eagles breast which has the moniker, **"belly button"**. They are known to occur on 1884 O, 1885 O, 1887 O, 1888 O, 1890 O, 1891 P, 1891 O, 1900 O, 1901 O and 1902 O, but usually don't affect the coin's value.

Rotated Dies

A striking error related to press adjustment errors is the so-called **rotated reverse**, when the reverse of a coin is not in the normal upside down position when a coin is turned over from the obverse side. This can occur when the dies were first installed in the coining press or later when they became loose. Rotations of **5 to 10 degrees** are **fairly common** and up to **15 degrees rotation** is considered **within normal tolerance**. However, usually rotated reverse coins of **45 to 180 degrees** clockwise or counterclockwise are the **ones that bring premium prices**. Collectible rotated reverse coins of 45 or more degrees are **fairly rare**. The **1878 CC** is the **most frequently found** rotated reverse with the

1888 O the next most frequently found. The following chart lists the known dates with rotated reverse, their VAM variety, rotation range and highest condition availability.

Mis-Fed Planchets

Planchets not fed properly into the collar and centered between the dies can result in some rare and spectacular striking error coins. Most noticeable are coins struck once **off-center out of the collar** with part of the design missing and a blank area on the opposite side of the coin. Large off-center coins of 20% or more bring large premiums, are **very rare** and most have been found and are part of collections. Coins **struck on center but out of the collar** with no reeding are called **broadstruck** because they are usually larger than normal diameter without the collar constraints. They are also quite rare for Morgan dollars. A related error is the **partial collar** where only some edge reeding is next to the coin reverse. A band of smooth edge without reeding next to the obverse has the moniker "**railroad rim**" because of the resemblance to a flanged railroad wheel.

Another type of mis-fed planchet error is the **double struck coin** where the first strike on a coin is not ejected and a second strike occurs over the first strike. Large shifts in the second strike are very rare and can be very spectacular and bring enormous premiums. Lesser shifts of the second strike bring correspondingly reduced premiums but are still rare. Only one example is known for the Morgan dollars of a planchet that was fed over a struck coin and then was struck on top of the coin. This created a so-called **capped** and dished obverse against the upper die and a reverse **enlarged incuse brockage** image on the other side where it was forced against the first struck coin obverse. A **unique** Morgan dollar error coin worth a **very high premium.**

Struck Thru Errors

All kinds of foreign material has been reported to be struck by the dies over the planchet for Morgan dollars. Most common are struck thru **grease** from the coining presses that makes **smooth indents** into the coin surface. That can enlarge and slowly disappear on several coins struck in sequence. Stray **wires** from cleaning brushes, **cloth** material, **threads**, **hair**, **scrap** and **silver strips** have been found to be struck thru on Morgan coins, usually on the **reverse lower die**. Struck thru coins usually have shiny smooth surfaces rather than the rough dark impure metal streaks. Only the large visible struck thru have much of a premium price.

Machine Doubling

Looseness and wear of the coin press parts can cause the dies to move laterally or bounce during the striking of the coin. This machine doubling always results in the **reduction** of portions of the raised normal design edges since the die moved sideways over the initial die impression. Die doubling on the other hand, always **enlarges** the design width since the hub moves laterally in the die cavity. Also machine doubling has **flat, shiny, shelf-like surfaces** raised only slightly above the coin's field. Die doubling has **dull rounded** and raised surfaces. Machine doubling usually will vary slightly from coin to coin struck by a given pair of dies as the dies moved slightly differently with each coin struck. Die doubling is the same for the coins struck by a given die pair.

The **reverse** of the coin **most commonly has machine doubling** for the Morgan dollar and was the lower die that frequently moved against the **worn die stake**. A reverse die could bounce during the striking of the coin creating a flat shiny doubling on portions of the design edges. Or sometimes the upper **obverse die moved sideways** during the coin striking **into the denticle edges** that created **machine doubling on the date digits** or adjacent stars upper edges. Since machine doubling is very common on Morgan dollars and differs on each struck coin, there is **no premium price** on this type of coin doubling. Rather it is a **confusing nuisance** when trying to determine if true die doubling exists on the coin.

Because the mint mark was punched into the reverse die after the design had been hubbed in, it can show die doubling but not the adjacent design. Machine doubling at the reverse lower mint mark area can be confusing if it shows as flat shiny doubling on the mint mark. Always check to see if there is also flat shiny machine doubling on the adjacent design to make sure the doubling on a mint mark is true die doubling from mis-aligned punch blows and not machine doubling.

Available references–

Comprehensive Catalog and Encyclopedia of Morgan & Peace Dollars, by Leroy C Van Allen & A. George Mallis, 4th ed., 1998, WorldWide Ventures, Chapter 7, Discussion of Significant Varieties.

1921 D Weak Strike

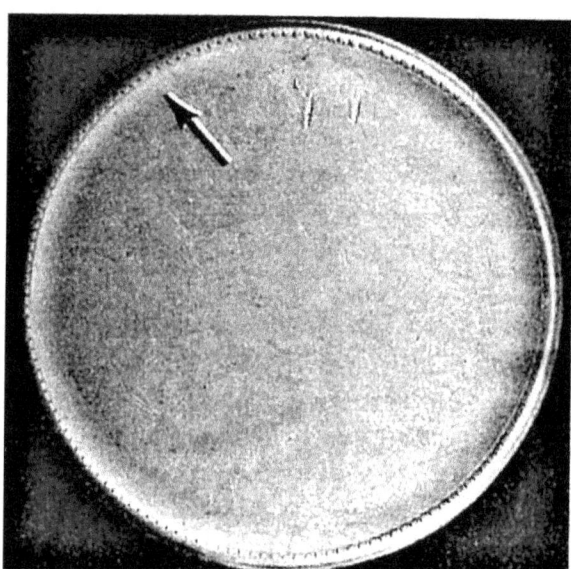

Partial Edge Denticles

1881 S Round Rim

1894 O Misaligned Die

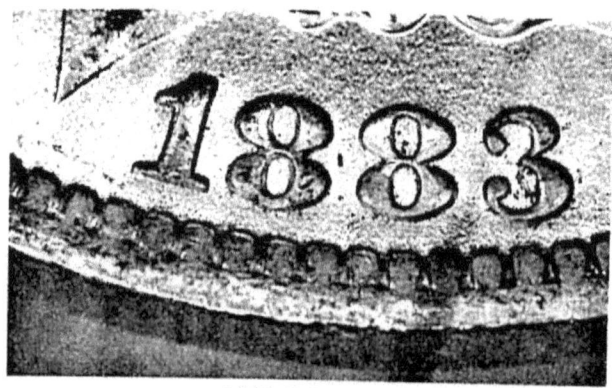

1883 O Square Rim

1885 O Belly Button

Flat Eagle's Breast

Flat Hair Over Ear

Rotated Reverse Dies

Date	Variety	Rotation	Highest Condition Availability
1878 CC	22	26-95° CW	BU
1883 O	1	32-77° CCW	BU
1886 O	4	15-48° CW	AU
	11	33-52° CCW	AU
1887 P	27	67-165° CW	Circulated
	27	80-140° CCW	AU
1888 O	9	15-28° CW & 15-175° CCW	BU
1889 P	18A	20° CCW	BU
1889 O	1	60-105° CW	Circulated
	3	23-73° CW	AU
	9	25-47° CW	Circulated
1890 O	8	36° CCW	Circulated
	23	20-60° CW	BU
1891 O	8	50-120° CCW	Circulated
1894 O	6A	25° CCW	Circulated
1901 O	46	76° CCW	AU
1904 O	13	24-46° CCW	BU
	18	62-69° CCW	BU
	40	59-128° CCW	BU
1921 P	45	45° CCW	BU
1921 Peace	?	60° CW, 20° CCW	?
1922 P	1	16° CCW	AU
	2BA	40° CW	AU
	?	100° CCW	?
1922 D	2	40-56° CW	BU
1923 P	1	25-100° CW	BU
1927 D	?	15° CW	?

1879 P Broadstruck

1901 S Broadstruck

1878 S 10% Off-Center K11

1880 S 30% Off-Center K1

1921 S 50% Off-Center K6

1900 O Partial Collar

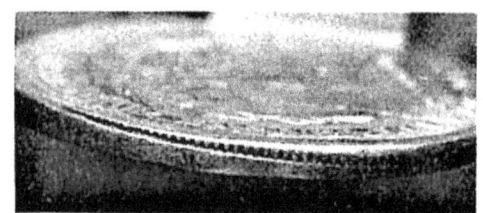

1921 S Tilted Partial Collar

1892 P Doubled/Quadrupled Struck Coin

1921 P Doubled Struck

1887 P Double Struck Obverse

1887 P Doubled Struck Reverse

1888 O Doubled Struck Obverse

1888 O Double Struck Reverse

1886 Capped Obverse

1886 Brockage Reverse

1881 P Obverse Struck Thru Grease, Normal Reverse

1896 P Imbedded Wire

1881 CC Struck Thru Scrap

1880 S Struck Thru

1921 P Struck-Thru Coin Fragment

1897 P Struck Thru Scrap

1921 P Struck Thru Grease

1921 S VAM 11 Struck Thru Grease

1921 S VAM 11 Struck Thru Grease

1921 P VAM 3 Machine Doubling

1921 P VAM 3 Machine Doubling

1921 P VAM 3 Machine Doubling

FURTHER REFERENCES

Please check Amazon Kindle for Michael S. Fey, Ph.D., and Leroy Van Allen & A. George Mallis publications. For hard copy print of books, please contact Dr. Fey at RCI, P.O. Box C, Ironia, NJ 07845 or eMail: Feyms@aol.com.

Hard copy books are also available at *The Institute for Silver Dollar Education and Research*, at website: *Ilovesilver dollars.org* or by contacting Executive Director John Baumgart at John.Baumgart@comcast.net

Amazon Kindle

Fey, Michael S. 2019. *The Complete Virtual Guide to Pricing Your Morgan Silver Dollars*. 286 pp. RCI

Van Allen, Leroy, & A. George Mallis. 2023. *Part I or II or III of Three. Comprehensive Catalog and Encyclopedia or Morgan & Peace Dollars*. RCI Total 520 pp.

Leroy Van Allen. 2011. *Wonders of Morgan Dollars*. 139 pp. RCI

Leroy Van Allen. 2013. *Wonders of Peace Dollars*. 273 pp. RCI

Leroy Van Allen. 2006. *Morgan Dollars 8 & 7 Over 8 Tail Feather Story*. 52 pp. RCI

Leroy Van Allen. 2010. *1878 P 7 Tail Feather Morgan Dollar Attribution Guide*. 130 pp. RCI

Leroy Van Allen. 2006. *1878 S Morgan Dollar Attribution Guide*. 139 pp. RCI

Fey, Michael S. 2009 The Top 100 Morgan Dollar Varieties: The VAM Keys

FURTHER REFERENCES

Hard Copy Books

Fey, Michael S. 2019. The Top 100 Morgan Dollar Varieties: The VAM Keys. 286 pp. RCI

Fey, Michael S. 2008. *A Decade of Top 100 Insights*. RCI 174 pp.

Van Allen, Leroy. 1991. *RotaFlip Die Rotation Booklet and Guide*. 1991. RCI

Kimpton, M.D., Mark. 2005. *Elite Clashed Morgan Dollars*. RCI 160 pp

Van Allen, Leroy, & A. George Mallis. 2023. *Comprehensive Catalog and Encyclopedia or Morgan & Peace Dollars*. RCI Total 520 pp.

Van Allen, Leroy 2011. *Wonders of Morgan Dollars*. 139 pp. RCI

Van Allen, Leroy 2013. *Wonders of Peace Dollars*. 273 pp. RCI

Van Allen, Leroy 2006. *Morgan Dollars 8 & 7 Over 8 Tail Feather Story*. 52 pp. RCI

Van Allen, Leroy 2010. *1878 P 7 Tail Feather Morgan Dollar Attribution Guide*. 130 pp. RCI

Van Allen, Leroy 2006. *1878 S Morgan Dollar Attribution Guide*. 139 pp. RCI

Van Allen, Leroy 2013. *Die Gouges and Scratches Peace Dollar Attribution Guide*. 109 pp RCI

Van Allen, Leroy 2008. *1921 Scribbles Morgan Dollar Attribution Guide*. 234 pp. RCI

Van Allen, Leroy. 2013. *Misplaced Date Digits Morgan Dollar Attribution Guide*. 57 pp RCI

Van Allen, Leroy. 2017. *Dashed Under 8 Morgan Dollar Attribution Guide*. 53 pp. RCI

Van Allen, Leroy. 2009. *Overdates and Over Mint Marks of Morgan Dollar Attribution Guide*. 53 pp. RCI

Van Allen, Leroy. 2015. *Denticle & Die Impressions Morgan Dollar Attribution Guide*. 109 pp. RCI

Van Allen, Leroy. 2009. *1921 P Infrequently Reeded or Wide Reeding Morgan Dollar Attribution Guide*. 31 pp. RCI

Van Allen, Leroy. 2011 *Amazing Changing 1921 S VAM 1B Thorn Head Morgan Dollar*. 2011. 22 pp. RCI

Van Allen, Leroy. 2009. *1889 P Doubled Ear Morgan Dollar Attribution Guide*. 32 pp. RCI

Van Allen, Leroy. 2016. *Micro o and Other Counterfeit Morgan and Peace Dollars*. 191 pp RCI

Van Allen, Leroy. 2005. *Micro o Mint Mark on Morgan Dollars*. 32 pp. RCI

Van Allen, Leroy. 2005. *Die Markers for 1921 Morgan and Peace Proof Dollars*. 9 pp. RCI

Van Allen, Leroy and Baumgart, John. 1992-Date Various VAM Book Yearly Supplements. RCI

www.ingramcontent.com/pod-product-compliance
Lightning Source LLC
Chambersburg PA
CBHW041513120626
46551CB00018B/2410